Europe's Coming
Demographic Challenge

Europe's Coming Demographic Challenge

Unlocking the Value of Health

Nicholas Eberstadt and Hans Groth

The AEI Press

Publisher for the American Enterprise Institute

WASHINGTON, D.C.

2007

Distributed to the Trade by National Book Network, 15200 NBN Way, Blue Ridge Summit, PA 17214. To order call toll free 1-800-462-6420 or 1-717-794-3800. For all other inquiries please contact the AEI Press, 1150 Seventeenth Street, N.W., Washington, D.C. 20036 or call 1-800-862-5801.

Library of Congress Cataloging-in-Publication Data

Eberstadt, Nick, 1955-
  Europe's coming demographic challenge : unlocking the value of health / by Nicholas Eberstadt and Hans Groth.
     p. cm.
Includes bibliographical references.
  ISBN-13: 978-0-8447-7200-4 (pbk.)
  ISBN-10: 0-8447-7200-3
  1. Europe—Population—Economic aspects. 2. Age distribution (Demography)—Europe. 3. Population aging--Europe. I. Groth, Hans. II. Title.

    HB3581.A3E24 2007
    304.6'1094—dc22

                                                        2007040264

11 10 09 08 07   1 2 3 4 5

Printed in the United States of America

Contents

List of Illustrations

TABLE

Acknowledgments

This publication was made possible by a grant from the German Marshall Fund of the United States (GMFUS). The authors would like to thank GMFUS for this generosity. In addition, Nicholas Eberstadt would like to offer grateful acknowledgment of Pfizer's longstanding support for his research in demography, health, and development.

Earlier versions of this study were presented to workshops at Baur au Lac in Zurich; at the Berlin Insitit für Bevölkerung und Entwicklung (BIBE) in Berlin; and at Instituto Bruno Leoni (IBL) in Milan. This monograph is the better for the many suggestions and constructive criticisms offered at those sessions. In particular, the authors would like to recognize professors Kurt Schildknecht and Peter Zweifel for their insightful suggestions and valuable comments on an earlier draft of this essay. Thanks are also due to Mr. Mark Keese of the Organisation for Economic Co-operation and Development (OECD) for generously providing unpublished data for our use. Finally, we would like to salute Ms. Megan Davy of the American Enterprise Institute for her invaluable research assistance. The opinions expressed here, and any remaining errors, are the authors' alone.

1

The Demographic Challenge to European Prosperity

In the past generation, Western Europe has fallen ever further behind the United States in our long-term transatlantic economic competition. Between 1980 and 2005, America's total growth in gross domestic product (GDP) outpaced OECD Europe's by an average of 0.8 percent per year.[1] For the period after 1995, America's annual tempo of economic growth exceeded Germany's—Europe's largest economy—by more than one percentage point a year, both in the aggregate and in per-capita terms.[2] Many factors have contributed to this widening gap and to the underlying gradual economic deceleration in Europe, which lies at the heart of the divide. The role of social and economic policies, for example, can hardly be ignored. But demographic trends also have had a major influence on the disparate American and European economic records over the past quarter-century. And the demographic divergence between Europe and America stands to be even more striking over the coming quarter-century.

If Europeans hope to remain economically competitive in the years ahead—or, perhaps more importantly, if they wish to enjoy continuing improvements in living standards and economic well-being—they must face these new demographic realities squarely, capitalizing upon thus-far ignored opportunities where they can, compensating for adverse population changes where they must.

Contrary to what some alarmed voices have been proclaiming in recent years, we maintain that the economic implications of Europe's demographic outlook over the next generation are by no means unremittingly bleak, despite the obvious challenges they

1

pose. For there are positive as well as negative demographic trends at work in Europe today, shaping the region's future. Most importantly on the positive side of the ledger, Europe appears extremely well-positioned to take advantage of the "healthy aging" of its population, as its workers exhibit great potential to remain productive at advanced ages—perhaps even greater potential, indeed, than their American counterparts.

Capitalizing upon the promise in Europe's impending demographic shifts, however, will require important—indeed, fundamental—changes, both in the way people think and in the ways they choose to live.

FIGURE 2-3
THE AGE DISTRIBUTION OF GREAT INNOVATION

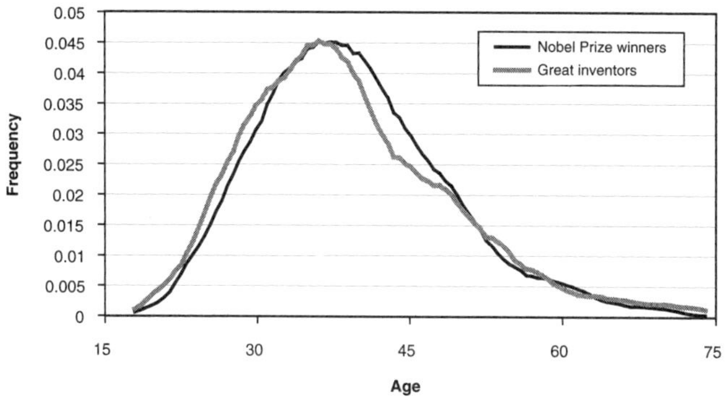

SOURCE: Benjamin F. Jones, "Age and Great Invention" (Working Paper 11359, National Bureau of Economic Research, May 2005), http://www.nber.org/papers/11359 (accessed July 2, 2007).

to decline, but much more modestly, while the total number of thirty-somethings and young forty-somethings will continue to grow, by an estimated 8 percent, between 2005 and 2030.)

One may, of course, argue that the physical "location" of knowledge-creators matters ever less in an internet-connected world economy; great inventions will benefit everyone, not just the country where a youthful innovator actually happens to live. But innovations in everyday business settings also matter; there are always mundane and immediate challenges that the global flow of knowledge cannot directly address, that must be dealt with locally—and may be dealt with better by people in those historically peak creative ages.[3]

And other economic problems beckon as well, due to Europe's brave new demography. One portentous but seldom-discussed matter relates to the youngest of the young adults.

In an information- and knowledge-intensive economy, education and training are absolutely critical to improving productivity. In modern societies, it is conventionally those young people fifteen to twenty-four years of age who imbue the latest training, through secondary and vocational schools, universities, and apprenticeships; for each new rising cohort, levels of technical and educational attainment tend to be more advanced.

But the stream of new trainees for Western Europe is starting to dry up. The situation is especially acute in Germany. A generation ago (1980) German youths fifteen to twenty-four years of age numbered 12.6 million; a generation from now (in 2030) projections are for just 7.4 million—a precipitous 41 percent drop![4] A generation ago, Germany had 172 rising fifteen- to twenty-four-year-olds as "replacement manpower" for every 100 people ages fifty-five to sixty-four; by 2030, that ratio will have fallen to just 65 rising youths for every 100 older men and women of working age. Similarly, in 2030 the prospective ratio of younger manpower to older manpower looks to be 63:100 in Greece; 64:100 in Austria; 61:100 in Spain; and a mere 52:100 in Italy. For Switzerland, the corresponding ratio in 2030 will not be that much better: Census Bureau projections suggest a total of 71 rising fifteen- to twenty-four-year-olds for every 100 persons fifty-five to sixty-four years old—and a ratio roughly the same as for Western Europe as a whole.

Thus, for Europe in general, improvement of overall levels of educational attainment within the labor force through the familiar everyday process of elder retirements and youthful recruits is steadily becoming a slower and more tentative dynamic than in the past—or than in America in the future, where the prospective ratio of those ages fifteen to twenty-four to those ages fifty-five to sixty-four looks to remain above or near 120:100 through the year 2030.

3

Europe's Limited Demographic Options

Surveying the demographic horizon, the outlook for Western Europe seems decidedly clouded. But it is *not* desperate or disastrous, let us emphasize. Such adjectives might be suitable for describing the parlous straits of the Russian Federation, where rapid population decline is being driven by an unremitting health catastrophe that has pushed overall Russian life expectancy down to, or even below, the levels prevailing in India. According to U.S. Census Bureau projections, overall life expectancy in 2007 is lower in Russia than in India; the UN Population Division sees rough parity in overall life expectancy between those two states today and envisions higher levels for India than for Russia over the decades ahead. And if Western Europe is unsettled by the prospect of a future demographic decline, Russia's real existing shift puts those projected trends in a sobering perspective: In percentage terms, Russia's *current* pace of depopulation is nearly three times higher than Western Europe's projected tempo for the year 2030.[1]

While Western Europe's impending demographic troubles look minimal in light of Russia's travails, we must recognize that population trends in Western Europe over the coming generation promise to complicate, rather than facilitate, the quest to maintain or improve the region's pace of economic growth—to constrain, rather than expand, possibilities for enhancing prosperity and promoting mass affluence.

A closer look at population projections can help us better appreciate what lies within the realm of the demographically possible for Europe—and how these limits and opportunities bear upon prospects for European competitiveness and well-being over the coming generation.

In 2005 (the most recent year for which data are available) Western Europe's annual death totals had come almost to match new births: By the reckoning of Eurostat, the European Community's statistical service, the region as a whole recorded just over eleven births for every ten deaths that year.[2] The "crossover point" at which deaths come to exceed births in Europe lies immediately before us. By the projections of the U.S. Census Bureau, that momentous switchover will occur in 2007; Eurostat, for its part, anticipates the event may not take place for another few years, possibly even as far into the future as 2013.[3] Irrespective of its precise date, however, all projections agree that Western Europe is poised for an imminent transition to a "net-mortality society," after which deaths will surpass births more or less permanently.

Between 2007 and 2030, Census Bureau projections expect Western Europe to see roughly 14.9 million more deaths than births; by the year 2030, in this vision of the future, there will be four deaths for every three births in Western Europe—and, in Germany, five deaths for every three births. In the United States, by contrast, the year 2030 is expected to herald three births for every two deaths.

Western Europe's population totals are envisioned as being kept in rough balance over the coming generation through immigration—with a net inflow of roughly 16.7 million newcomers over this period. By 2030, the presumed net inflow of immigrants into Western Europe would be averaging somewhat under 700,000 a year, down from around 750,000 a year in 2007. Given Europe's impending and widening imbalance between births and deaths, this continuing stream of newcomers would not prevent the region's eventual population decline, but it would serve to postpone the onset of negative growth by nearly a decade and a half. As already noted, deaths are projected to exceed births in Western Europe very soon; the projected immigration trends for the region would contribute to continuing, if marginal, population growth through 2020, with overall declines in total numbers commencing in 2021. By 2030, despite envisioned immigration, this projection expects Western Europe's population to be shrinking at a tempo of over half a million persons a year.

These projections are, of course, just that—merely projections. They are based upon assumed trends in the future, and can therefore be challenged or disputed.[4] If we examine the particulars that have gone into them, we can, as is always true for projections, quibble with certain specifics, or offer our own preferred alternative assumptions. Yet perhaps the most powerful impression to be conveyed is just how unyielding some of the demographic trends now unfolding in Europe are likely to be. Simply stated, it promises to be extraordinarily difficult to alter Western Europe's fertility or immigration outlook to any appreciable degree—or, at least, to alter them appreciably over the coming generation.

Consider first the issue of fertility and births. Is it possible the projections in question may be understating the scope for birth resurgence in Western Europe? If this is the case, it is not because the U.S. Census Bureau posits a continuing slump in Western European fertility levels; those projections actually envision a limited increase in childbearing, from current levels of roughly 1.5 births per woman to a notional 1.6 births per woman in 2030. If current fertility levels prevail in 2030, Western Europe will see roughly a quarter-million fewer births than projected here; flat-lined fertility from the present through 2030 implies something like 2.5 million fewer births for Western Europe over the coming generation than the Census Bureau projections discuss.

The case for a coming upsurge in Western European fertility is adduced by some observers in what they see as the "existence proof" of relatively high levels of fertility that already prevail in one exemplary European society: France. In early 2007, France's National Institute for Statistics and Economic Studies (INSEE) reported that country's fertility may have been the highest in the entire European Union (EU) in 2005, with an estimated total fertility rate (TFR) of 1.94[5]—not so far below the TFR of 2.07 that would be necessary for long-term population replacement in a contemporary France.[6] INSEE further indicated that 2006 looked to be a bumper year for births in France, with the possibility that the TFR for the country as a whole might approach 2.0 for the first time in decades.

But is this French case "generalizable" to the rest of Europe? French scholars and commentators would be among the first to challenge such a proposition; French writing, after all, has long spoken of the special, even exceptional, nature of the French demographic experience.[7] (Indeed, even French president Nicolas Sarkozy has mentioned "L'exception française" in this regard.[8]) Moreover, France's seemingly high general fertility levels beg analysis and disaggregation by ethnicity and nationality, but this is virtually impossible, given the government's longstanding "republican" ideological refusal to collect or disseminate such statistical information. As a practical matter, such official restrictions make it exceedingly difficult to estimate France's immigrant and "native" populations.

One careful demographic attempt to penetrate France's opaque official presentation of statistics on fertility, nativity, and immigration estimated that nearly 20 percent of France's babies are currently born to immigrant mothers—and that the fertility rate for France's foreign parents stands around 40 percent above the national average.[9] Rough arithmetic suggests this would mean a TFR of about 1.7 for France's "native" population—including those whose parents had immigrated to France in the 1960s and 1970s. Viewed from this perspective, France's present "exceptional" fertility levels may not look quite so exceptional after all; the gap between fertility levels for "old France" and the rest of the EU (where TFRs are currently around 1.52) may still be meaningful, but rather less dramatic than is widely supposed nowadays.

Some might also raise a more technical point concerning the distinction demographers draw between "period" and "cohort" fertility rates. The former—used in conventional discussions—offer a sort of "snapshot" of childbearing patterns for women of all ages in a given calendar year, while the latter refer to completed levels of fertility for a particular group of women at the end of their childbearing years. There can occasionally be considerable differences between these "period" and "cohort" rates, and, indeed, one sees such a discrepancy in Western Europe today. Whereas the latest "snapshot" (that is, period) fertility data for, say, the EU-15 indicate a TFR of 1.54 for 2004, the completed (that is, cohort) TFR for women born in 1965—in other words those who are today at least forty years of age—is 1.72, or about 12 percent higher.[10] Some analysts believe this discrepancy may mean that today's Western European women are postponing babies they eventually intend to bear; this was the case in the United States in the 1970s, when "period" TFRs sank close to 1.7 before returning to 2.0 and above in the late 1980s.[11]

But a distinction between "period" and "cohort" fertility rates does not necessarily mean fertility levels will eventually be heading up; it can also mean that family formation patterns for younger women are changing. And there is ample evidence that dramatic, even radical, changes in family patterns have been underway in Western Europe in the past generation. In the three decades between 1975 and 2004, the EU-15's "total first marriage rate" (the odds that a woman will marry before the age of fifty) fell by over thirty percentage points—from 88 percent to just 57 percent—while the "total divorce rate" (the odds of divorcing before age fifty) more than doubled, from 17 percent to 36 percent.[12] And this "second demographic transition," as some term it, continues its advance throughout Western Europe. In Germany, to pick just one country, the total first marriage rate dropped during the 1995–2004 decade to just 55 percent, while the total divorce rate climbed to 46 percent.[13] All else being equal, less stable marital unions would be expected to conduce to smaller families, not a fertility upswing.

And what about population policy? Here the historical record is fairly clear: Pronatalist policies are expensive and of extremely limited long-term efficacy. Sudden new birth bonuses and subventions can change parents' timing decisions, but in industrial and postindustrial societies, they are most unlikely to alter desired family size to any great degree. A careful recent study by two French economists proclaimed what they saw as the potentialities of pronatalist family policy, but their vision of success would be regarded by most of the rest of us as failure. In their conjectural estimates, tens of billions of euros per year in additional subventions for additional children in France *might* raise total fertility rates by 0.1 birth per woman per lifetime.[14] If they are correct, such an approach, at vast expense, would offer scant mitigation for Western Europe's "birth dearth" over the coming generation.

Now, what about immigration? Here again, at the moment, Western Europe looks as if it is stuck with a rather narrow band of options.

On the one hand, all else being equal, significantly reducing the net inflow of newcomers to the European space looks likely to be serious economic folly, since immigration postpones the onset of population decline and slows the region's pace of population aging. The extreme case can be indicated by "contrafactual" population projections assuming zero immigration between now and 2030. Changing no other parameters, the zero migration scenario would reduce total population in 2030 for the EU-15 by about 27 million; the working-age population would be almost 20 million smaller than otherwise projected. The ratio of sixty-five-plus to twenty- to sixty-four-year-olds would rise to 44 percent (as against 41 percent under existing projections), and the proportion of senior citizens sixty-five and older would likewise be higher than otherwise projected (26.5 percent versus 25.1).[15] Less dramatic cutbacks in immigration would have more limited consequences but would nevertheless reinforce these very same tendencies toward demographic graying and shrinking.

On the other hand, all else being equal, increasing the existing flows of immigration to Europe promises to be problematic for an entirely different set of reasons. Plainly stated, Europe has not yet devised a workable formula for assimilating newcomers from overseas into productive and loyal citizens of the EU or the localities in question.

This is not, of course, to deny the many "success stories" in recent waves of immigration into Western Europe, either on an individual or a mass level. Indeed, much of what one does not hear about in Western European media today are the ways in which the majority of newcomers are working hard in—and working hard to fit into—the countries receiving them. Nevertheless, with Islamist radicalism and other currently less extreme problems already in evidence among Western European immigrants (or their children), the continuation of historical postwar patterns of migration into Western Europe (much less an acceleration of such flows) would pose major questions about social cohesion and perhaps even domestic security—questions that, at least for the moment, Western European societies are clearly not capable of answering.

Moreover, all things are not likely to hold equal with the interactions between changing immigration flows and Western European economic performance. Some of the issues in play may be imponderables for now, but consequential and self-reinforcing in the years ahead.

The educational and entrepreneurial caliber of immigrants entering Europe in the decades ahead, for example, is hardly a fixed and unchanging demographic parameter. (A spirit of innovation and dynamism attracts highly skilled young migrants, just as economic stagnation and sclerosis tends to fend them away; talented and trained Asians may beat a path from Bangalore and Beijing to Silicon Valley these days, but relatively few indicate continental Europe as a first choice.) The presumption that young immigrants will stoke Europe's economic engines, furthermore, pivots on the premise that these newcomers will be successfully integrated into society and the workforce in the receiving countries; but it is possible to imagine circumstances under which the link between immigration and productivity could be strained, or even severed, for particular waves of new entrants to Europe.

And foreign immigration could have its own impact on the disposition of native-born Europeans to consider migrating themselves. By and large, Western European statistical systems are not well-equipped these days to tabulate emigration of the native-born, but the era of European emigration is not entirely behind us.

According to first estimates, for example, the Netherlands experienced a net *out-migration* of population in 2005—that is, the year after the shocking and widely followed Islamist murder of filmmaker Theo Van Gogh.[16] And even two years earlier—in 2003, when Holland was still registering a net inflow of migrants—official statistics suggested that as many as 80,000 Dutch nationals were moving out of their homeland each year. The overwhelming majority of those leaving the Netherlands, incidentally, were people of working age (twenty to sixty-four years old)—and the peak emigration cohort happened to be those prime younger adults between the ages of twenty-five and thirty-nine.[17]

There is strong reason to believe, furthermore, that contemporary Europe's out-migrants are not only disproportionately self-selected from the prime working-age cohorts, but that they also tend to be better educated and more highly skilled than the peers they leave behind. This much is suggested by comparing data on the educational profiles of the working-age populations of Western Europe, on the one hand, and of émigrés from those same countries who currently live in the United States, on the other (see table 3-1).

Around the year 2000, for virtually every country in Western Europe, the proportion of the adult population with college or graduate training was higher—and, typically, substantially higher—for those expatriates now residing in the United States than it was in the country of origin. In most cases, the proportion of U.S.-based Europeans with higher training was reportedly at least half again as high as in their native land—and, in some cases, the differentials were even more dramatic.[18] Whereas in France, for example, just 23 percent of the population ages twenty-five to sixty-four had attained tertiary education,[19] the corresponding proportion for French-born adults living in the United States was nearly 52 percent—almost thirty percentage points higher. The proportion of Austrian adults with higher education was nearly three times higher for those living in America (38 percent) than for those who had not left their homeland (14 percent). No less striking, in its way, is the contrast between education levels for locals and emigrants from affluent Switzerland, one of Europe's most affluent and productive societies: Whereas 26 percent of Swiss adults had attained tertiary education, in the United States that share was 54 percent, over twice as high. Dramatic as all these differences appear, moreover, there is reason to suspect that the figures in table 3-1 may actually *understate* the educational differences that characterize Western Europeans who are prompted to migrate out of Europe today and those who remain behind.[20]

TABLE 3-1
EDUCATIONAL ATTAINMENT FOR THE ADULT POPULATION:
WESTERN EUROPE, THE UNITED STATES, AND WESTERN EUROPEAN
EMIGRANTS RESIDING IN THE UNITED STATES, C. 2000

	Educational attainment of population ages 25–64 by country (percent)			Educational attainment of foreign-born ages 25+ living in the U.S. by country of origin (percent)
	Below upper secondary	Upper secondary and post-secondary	Tertiary	Tertiary
Austria	24.3	61.8	13.9	37.9
Belgium	41.5	31.4	27.1	46.7
Denmark	19.8	53.7	26.5	47.6
Finland	26.2	41.5	32.3	51.8
France	36.1	40.6	23	51.8
Germany	17.4	59.4	23.2	33.7
Greece	48.6	33.6	17.8	23.5
Ireland	42.4	22	35.6	30
Italy	56.7	33.2	10	17
Luxembourg	47.3	34.6	18.1	39.8
Netherlands	45	32	22.2	44.8
Portugal	80.1	10.8	9	10.4
Spain	59.7	16.2	23.6	38.2
Sweden	19.4	49	31.6	51.2
United Kingdom	37.1	36.9	26.1	42
Iceland (2001)	36	39	25	47
Norway (2001)	15	56	29	43.5
Switzerland (2001)	12	62	26	53.8
EU-15	38.9	37.3	23.8	
United States	12.3	50.3	37.3	

SOURCES: André Sapir et al., *An Agenda for a Growing Europe: The Sapir Report* (New York: Oxford University Press, 2004), table 4.4, p. 40; U.S. Census Bureau, "United States Foreign-Born Population: Foreign-Born Profiles," available online at http://www.census.gov/population/www/socdemo/foreign/datatbls.html; OECD, *Education at a Glance: OECD Indicators, 2002* (Paris: OECD, 2002), table A3.1a, p. 51.

NOTE: Definitions of educational levels here are from the International Standard Classification of Education (ISCED-97); for the U.S. educational system, "tertiary education" would include not only graduate study and a bachelor's degree, but also training for an associate's degree.

Already by the 1990s, quiet out-migration by native-born Western Europeans amounted to rather more than a trickle. According to the 2000 census, at the turn of the century over 600,000 U.S. residents were emigrants from the eighteen countries of Western Europe who had reportedly entered the United States during the decade 1990–99 alone. (The utterly overwhelming majority of these migrants, incidentally, were classified as "white" under America's statistical taxonomy, suggesting that the proportion of immigrants counted within this flow who were originally from Asia, Africa, and elsewhere but "reimmigrated" from Europe to the United States was very small indeed).[21]

When one considers that the United States is by no means the only potential venue for emigrating Europeans, it might prove that an overall total of close to one million "natives" from Western Europe moved out of the continent of their birth during the comparatively tranquil decade of the 1990s.

It is by no means unreasonable to expect the propensity of Western Europeans to emigrate to be affected by perceptions of domestic social stability or assessments of the local economic outlook—quantities that could in turn be affected, either positively or negatively, by immigration flows and the attendant socioeconomic record regarding assimilation. This is no longer a matter of pure conjecture; recent research has helped to quantify some of the contours for this relationship in modern-day Europe.

Survey data for the Netherlands from the year 2005, for example, indicate that respondents who were giving serious thought to moving abroad tended disproportionately to be concerned with such issues as "system of law and order," "crime level," "mental outlook of the people," "ethnic diversity," "noise pollution," and other worries that are today typically associated in Western Europe with assimilation troubles in immigrant communities. Significantly, these data suggest that a change in thinking about emigration may be underway in contemporary Europe—namely, the impulse for out-migration may be influenced less today than in the past by such traditional factors as economic calculation, and more by considerations bearing on quality of life, including perceptions of law and order or personal safety. Ominously, these recent Dutch data indicate that many of the (by and large young and well-educated) citizens giving serious thought to moving abroad would actually be willing to do so even if this meant a decline in their incomes, so long as it also meant they would not have to live with the social problems that were bothering them at home.[22]

In April 2005, nearly a third of Dutch respondents in one survey reported they had given thought to moving abroad.[23] This extraordinary result can be interpreted in very different ways: as a passing epiphenomenon in a European nation already exceptionally open to the notion of international movement, or as a foretaste of a particular variant of a more general European future. In any case, when it comes to the outlook for migration for Western Europe, it may suffice for now to observe that a presumption of zero emigration of the native-born from the region over the coming generation is entirely unwarranted—as is the assumption that native emigration and foreign immigration should be regarded as entirely unrelated tendencies.

The existence of such potentially complex interrelationships only underscores the difficulty European societies may have in attempting to "fine-tune" migration flows in the service of economic development over the coming generation, whether to increase or decrease these influxes of newcomers. Although migration law, unlike family size, is a prerogative of state sovereignty, in practice Western Europe may have scarcely more latitude in purposely altering its migration flows than its birthrates.

4

Healthy Aging: An Economic Trump Card?

Fortunately for Western Europe, there is one important demographic realm, critical to productivity and economic competitiveness, in which the region possesses a clear and compelling
"comparative advantage": the area of mortality and health. Today,
however, Europe capitalizes upon the economic potential of this
advantage much less than it could. Unlocking the full value of
Western Europe's "health edge"—and maintaining this demographic
advantage over the coming generation—will be the key contribution
demography can make to enhancing prosperity and development
for Europeans over the years immediately ahead.

In the modern economy, growth is driven ever less by natural
resources and ever more by human resources. "Human capital" is the
indispensable ingredient to sustainable economic development—
and perhaps the central element in this complex quantity is health.
Health not only contributes directly to economic potential through
improved physical capabilities, but it facilitates the processes of
learning and skill retention that bear such high returns in the information age. All around the world today, health equals wealth.

We can see this basic truth underscored on a global scale if we
compare life expectancy at birth (the most vivid summary measure
of a population's overall mortality patterns)[1] with per-capita GDP
internationally (see figure 4-1). As is evident from this graphic, there
is a regular and fairly tight correspondence in the modern world
between a country's level of health, here represented by its average
life expectancy, and its economic potential—the higher the former,
the greater the latter is likely to be. Considering the tremendous
diversity of contemporary populations and governments, we might
suggest that the revealed relationship between health and wealth is

FIGURE 4-1

HEALTH EQUALS WEALTH: LIFE EXPECTANCY VS. PURCHASING POWER
PARITY PER CAPITA GDP

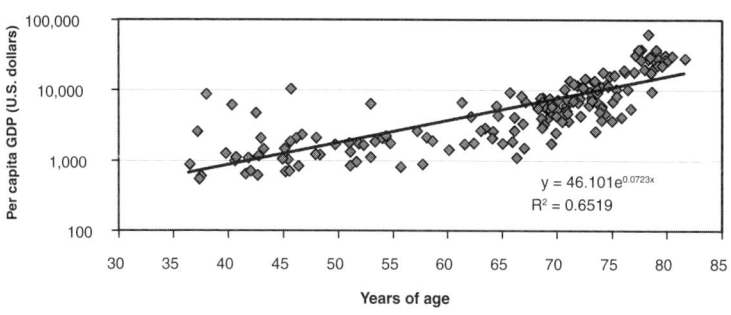

SOURCE: World Bank, *World Development Indicators, 2003* (Washington, D.C.: World Bank,
2003).
NOTE: Estimates are for the year 2001.

remarkably robust. To be sure, the relationship is by no means uni-
directional—wealth obviously promotes health, just as health helps
generate wealth—and the interplay between these two quantities
can be complex and subtle.[2] Yet at the end of the day, health turns
out to be a very good predictor for a society's level of productivity. For the world as a whole today, every additional year of life
expectancy is associated with roughly a 7 percent increase in per-
capita GDP. This powerful association witnessed across countries at
any given point in time, incidentally, is equally evident at the local
level, if we trace the relationship between health and wealth in given
countries or populations over time.

Happily for Western Europe, its peoples today enjoy a literally
vital demographic edge in health and mortality over almost all the
rest of the world. By almost any metric one might care to choose,
the general level of public health in Western Europe, by comparison with other regions of the planet, is exceptionally good. Most
noteworthy for our present purposes is that conditions of health

and longevity, on the whole, appear to be somewhat more favorable in Western Europe than in the United States.

The point is significant and merits some sustained attention. In 2003—the latest year for which fully comparable data are available for the United States and all of Western Europe—life expectancy at birth for American men was an estimated 74.7 years.[3] For the EU-15, the figure was 76.0 years, and for the other two major countries of Western Europe, Norway and Switzerland, the levels were 77.0 years and 77.9 years, respectively.[4] Among women an analogous gap was evident. Here, life expectancy at birth was 80.0 for the United States, 81.7 for the EU-15, 81.9 for Norway, and 83.9 for Switzerland. Overall, life expectancy was a year or so higher in "old Europe" than in America—and for Europe's healthiest (and, as it happens, wealthiest) countries, the gap was on the order of three to four years.

Parsing the data a bit more closely does not at all alter the basic picture. On a country-by-country basis, U.S. life expectancy at birth is not utterly below the levels seen today in Western Europe, but it is near the bottom, with only Portuguese men and Danish women reporting shorter lives. America is a famously multiethnic society, marked by equally famous ethnic disparities in health—yet even life expectancy for so-called "white" Americans does not rate particularly well in European comparisons. Of Western Europe's eighteen countries, fourteen national populations report higher male life expectancy and all eighteen report higher female life expectancy than are reported for contemporary American "whites."

From an international standpoint, U.S. survival schedules look best at the older ages—yet even here, American health outcomes would appear no better than mediocre in the Western European mirror. In the year 2003, for example, life expectancy at age sixty for American men was just about the same as the EU-15 average, while among women life expectancy was about half a year lower for Americans than for their EU-15 counterparts. In German-speaking Europe, incidentally, life expectancy at sixty was slightly higher in both Germany and Austria than in the United States by all the measures just mentioned, and Swiss survival schedules

FIGURE 4-2

HEALTHY LIFE EXPECTANCY: WESTERN EUROPE VS. UNITED STATES, 2002

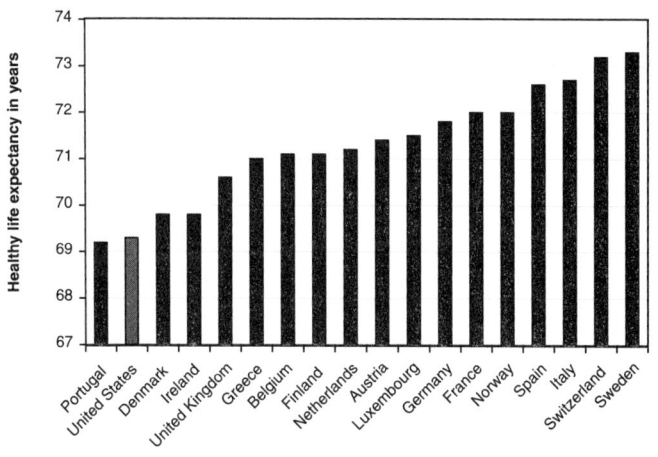

SOURCE: Organisation for Economic Co-operation and Development, *Society at a Glance: OECD Social Indicators, 2005 Edition* (Paris: OECD, 2005).

from virtually every vantage point were yet more favorable than the German.

The economic implications of these transatlantic mortality differentials may also be considered from the standpoint of health-adjusted life expectancy (HALE), a concept now favored by the World Health Organization (WHO). HALE proposes to measure the years of life spent free from disability and debilitating illnesses and afflictions—an important datum, although obviously also a difficult one to calculate with precision. Unlike life expectancy, there is no single and self-evident definition of HALE, and thus no single, universally accepted metric or procedure for estimating it. The issues entailed in compiling accurate and comparable HALE data are highly technical and far from trivial. But technical issues notwithstanding, WHO and OECD now offer estimates of HALE for the United States and Western Europe, and the calculations are striking (see figure 4-2 above).

For the year 2002, of all the Western European countries, only relatively poor Portugal is said to have a lower HALE than the United States. Overall, the populations of the EU-15 are estimated to enjoy significantly more years of "healthy life" than American citizens—indeed, an average of over two years more. These same numbers suggest that Germans can expect about two and a half more years of healthy life than Americans, while the Swiss can count on almost four years more.

In and of themselves, contemporary Western Europe's advantageous health and mortality conditions confer corresponding competitive advantages upon its populations in terms of current economic potential. But dynamic, long-term tendencies for enhancing productivity and economic growth can also emerge from these favorable health patterns.

Western European populations of economically active ages face distinctly better odds of surviving the working years than do Americans. Figure 4-3 underscores this important point. Under 2002 survival schedules, for example, a twenty-year-old American stood nearly an 18 percent risk of dying before age sixty-five. In Germany, by contrast, that risk was only about 14 percent—that is, one-fifth lower—and in Italy, Switzerland, and Sweden it was less than 12 percent, or just two-thirds of the U.S. level.

Why does this matter to long-term development prospects? Because training and higher education facilitate sustained productivity growth and material advance, and good health during the working ages encourages a deepening of the "human capital stock" in just such skills. Premature mortality and foreshortened lives have unforgiving implications for the cost-benefit calculus for young adults' additional investments in learning; all else being equal, longer and healthier life incentivizes the decision to invest in further instruction by making it less risky, less costly, and more profitable.[5]

Although it is now commonplace to bemoan Europe's demographic handicaps and disadvantages, the fact of the matter is that the European health and mortality profile is a tremendous blessing—and a potentially powerful economic springboard. Central

FIGURE 4-3
ODDS OF NOT SURVIVING FROM AGE 20 TO AGE 65:
WESTERN EUROPE VS. UNITED STATES

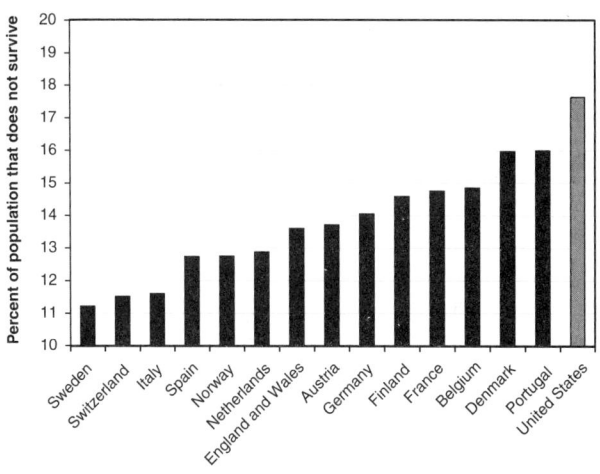

SOURCE: University of California, Berkeley and Max Planck Institute for Demographic Research, Human Mortality Database, http://www.mortality.org (accessed December 21, 2006).
NOTE: Based on age-specific mortality schedules for the year 2002.

to the interplay of demography and economics in Europe over the coming generation is the concept of "healthy aging."

Thanks to a phenomenon known as "the compression of morbidity," affluent societies the world over are finding that longer lifespans make for more vigorous and robust senior citizens. Studies on long-term data from the United States, for example, strongly suggest that the burden of disability and chronic disease has fallen markedly over the past century for American men in their fifties, sixties, and early seventies. Not only does the onset of such debilitating conditions seem to have been steadily postponed to ever later ages, but the prevalence of comorbidities or multiple afflictions also appears to have dropped very significantly over time.[6] There is reason to believe that the same trends would be seen for European populations if long-term data on health status for older cohorts were comparably available.[7]

Moreover, so far as can yet be determined, the benefits of "healthy aging" do not appear to stop with some given birthday, but instead extend across the entire course of life. Indeed, even among Europe's "oldest of the old," health and vitality appear to be increasing over time; in Germany, for example, survey data point to a steady decline in physical frailty and dependency upon caregivers among octogenarians and nonagenarians.[8]

And even better news regarding healthy aging and longevity may be on the horizon for the populations of Europe. Contrary to the long-held presumption that there are "fixed limits" to human life expectancy, a growing body of research is bringing evidence to bear for the proposition that there are no obvious and identifiable biological boundaries for male or female lifespans.

As this work documents, for over a century and a half the record life expectancy for the world's longest-lived country has been steadily rising—virtually at a steady linear pace of almost three months per calendar year. Further, there is as yet no indication of any deceleration in the annual pace of improvements for "frontrunner" countries, even though the top life expectancies in the world today are nearly four decades greater than those from 1850. In the words of two leading longevity researchers, "The linear climb of record life expectancy suggests that reductions in mortality should not be seen as a disconnected sequence of unrepeatable revolutions but rather as a regular stream of continuing progress."[9]

No less significant, death rates for the "oldest of the elderly"— octogenarians, nonagenarians, and even centenarians—though of course higher than for younger cohorts, have recorded similarly steady declines over time. In Sweden, France, England and Wales, and other developed societies, death rates for women in their eighties dropped by fully half between the mid-1950s and the mid-1990s[10]— and subsequent studies suggest that the tempo of mortality improvement among men and women in their eighties and nineties might actually have been picking up somewhat in recent years.[11] In other words, there is no sign yet of an approach to biological constraints against improvements in survival prospects, even for the very oldest members of society. Considered in tandem with the evidence for the compression of morbidity, these data suggest that the odds of being both alive and healthy in later life have been steadily increasing over time, especially for the world's more affluent societies.

To be very clear: We wish to emphasize that there is nothing preordained or inevitable about the continuing improvement of survival prospects and health conditions in Western Europe, or anywhere else. The terrible counterexample of modern-day Russia proves it is still possible for life expectancy and health to stagnate—or even deteriorate—for decades on end in a literate, urban European society during times of peace.

Moreover, even in the more affluent OECD societies, inexorable health progress is hardly to be taken for granted. In the United States, for example, recent survey data offer some troubling signs about the health status of Americans now approaching retirement. According to one analysis, American "boomers" in their early and mid-fifties in the year 2004 suffered distinctly more impairment in an array of everyday physical activities than did their counterparts just twelve years earlier. (To give just one example, whereas some 9 percent of American women ages fifty-one to fifty-six reported problems climbing a single flight of stairs in 1992, by 2004 the fraction was 14 percent).[12] It is possible these results are artifacts reflecting random sampling error or changes in survey design and technique rather than underlying trends among the populations in question.[13] Alternatively, they may speak to the very real consequences of genuine adverse phenomena such as rising levels of obesity—an epidemiological condition currently more extreme in the United States than in other industrialized societies, and apparently still worsening. We cannot yet be sure what these soundings portend for public health in America in the years immediately ahead. But as the issue of obesity should itself vividly underscore, there is no guarantee that higher incomes, improved education, and technological innovation will directly and in all cases translate into improved health behavior by an informed public in an open society.

Yet the demonstrated formula for methodically improving public health in affluent societies already exists and lies in our hands—and this "intricate interplay of advances in income, salubrity, nutrition, education, sanitation, and medicine" (in the words of Jim Oeppen and James W. Vaupel)[14] has made for continuing long-term improvements in health and mortality for those societies that have made use of it. If Western European societies and their governments continue to embrace and support this "intricate interplay," the possibility of significant or even major advances in health status for Europeans—including Europeans of ripe old age—should not be summarily discounted.

5

Enhancing Prosperity through Healthy Aging

The great economic opportunities opened by "healthy aging" do not, of course, pivot on the possibility of putting great-grandparents to work. Rather, they currently revolve around the prospects for eliciting greater productive activity from people enjoying a vigorous middle age—that is to say, men and women in their fifties and sixties (and maybe some in their seventies as well).

In all likelihood, the present generation of Western Europeans in their third quarter-century of life—that is to say, those currently ages fifty to seventy-four—is more physically robust and mentally alert than any preceding generation in the continent's entire history. It is also, from a technical and scientific standpoint, the most highly educated and best-trained generation of older men and women that the continent has ever seen.

Furthermore, thanks to the ongoing structural transformation of Europe's economy—knowledge-based, service-driven development—exhausting physical labor is no longer a job requirement in the typical Western European workplace. Modern Europe's work-tools are no longer the pickax, the wheelbarrow, and the loading dock; they are instead the office desk, the telephone, and the keyboard, a fundamentally auspicious "upgrade" from the standpoint of would-be older workers.

No less auspiciously, over the coming quarter-century we can expect the health and education of Europe's fifty- to seventy-four-year-olds to increase still further, while at the same time, ordinary work conditions will become ever less physically arduous for the average employee. All this augurs well for an upsurge in economic activity on the part of older Europeans—indeed, for a fundamental shift in the horizon over which older adults make net positive contributions to their national economies.

Research by Professor Ronald D. Lee of the University of California-Berkeley helps to elucidate the dimensions of this phenomenon. For a number of countries, Lee and his colleagues have carefully estimated both per-capita labor earnings and per-capita consumption at every year of age over the course of the entire life cycle. Their findings for the United States may suffice here for purposes of illustration (see figure 5-1). The dark gray line in the chart indicates average age-specific earnings; the black line, age-specific consumption. In the age groups where the dark gray line is higher than the black line, the population is producing a net earnings "surplus" above and beyond their own annual consumption. The total area of the space between the two points where the black and dark gray lines intersect suggests the size of the "labor surplus" generated during peak working years. That "surplus" may, in effect, be allocated to one's own consumption at later (or earlier) ages or may be applied to support the consumption of other people (for example, family members), or it may alternatively be used for savings and investment.

Perhaps surprisingly, in the United States in the year 2000, per-capita labor earnings exceeded per-capita consumption in the population at large only between the ages of twenty-five and fifty-eight—that is to say, for well under half of the expected lifespan of the current American citizen. Comparable figures are not yet available for contemporary Western European societies, but we might suspect that the percentage of total life years during which the average European citizen is a "net consumer" rather than a "net producer" is no lower than in the United States, and quite possibly is somewhat higher.

Capturing some of the economic opportunities inherent in "healthy aging" could be conceptualized here in terms of pushing back the typical lifetime "crossover point" at which consumption exceeds earnings, perhaps from the fifties to the sixties (or even, perhaps, the seventies)—and by smoothing the current subsequent drop-off in earnings at later ages onto a somewhat less precipitous trajectory.[1]

FIGURE 5-1
U.S. CONSUMPTION AND LABOR EARNINGS BY AGE, 2000

SOURCE: Ronald D. Lee, *Global Population Aging and Its Economic Consequences* (Washington, D.C.: AEI Press, 2007).
NOTE: Distinguishing private and public components (in kind transfers and prorated items like defense; cash benefits excluded).

In the aggregate, more individual earning power later in life would have at least two significant positive macroeconomic consequences. First, it would raise average overall purchasing power and, thus, in the immediate instance make for a more prosperous society. Second, it would increase the scope for locally financed savings and investment and, in so doing, could potentially accelerate the pace of long-term growth.

Note, in addition, that when societies move toward essentially stationary, zero-growth population structures—as Western Europe is now doing—the ages at which the average citizen commences and ceases to act as a "net economic producer" assume an increased salience in the performance of the macroeconomy. In such societies, in the absence of greater labor-force participation through "healthy aging," the main alternatives for achieving overall lifecycle balances between income and consumption are three: reduced consumption; reduced savings and investment, and thus slower growth; and reduced survival prospects for the elderly. Not exactly appealing options!

6

Europe's Ongoing Retreat from the Workplace

All in all, the economic case for "unlocking the value of health" in Europe through greater labor-force participation at older ages would appear persuasive—some might say powerful and compelling. Yet, most remarkably, over the course of a generation and more, Western Europeans have been translating all of their increased life expectancy into leisure time—and then some. For more than forty-five years, as life expectancy in Western Europe has steadily risen, average retirement ages have just as steadily fallen.

Trends in France—a case admittedly extreme even in the European context—illustrate the general tendency (see figure 6-1). Between the early 1960s and the turn of the century, male life expectancy in France rose by about eight years. Over the same period, the mean male retirement age fell by seven years. One need not be a demographer, or an actuary, to understand where this economic story is leading.

Of course, life expectancy and average age of retirement are not precisely comparable quantities; therefore, the arithmetic difference between these two quantities will not equal the average duration of retirement. But that great final vacation has been vastly extended in length throughout Western Europe in recent decades. Between 1970 and 2004, according to calculations by the OECD, the average expected length of retirement in France increased by nearly a decade for women, and over a decade for men, fully doubling pensioned life.[1] In Germany, the corresponding estimated increases were a decade for women and eight years for men; in Spain, eleven years and nine years, respectively. Today life expectancy in retirement exceeds

FIGURE 6-1
MALE RETIREMENT AGE VS. LIFE EXPECTANCY IN FRANCE, 1962–99

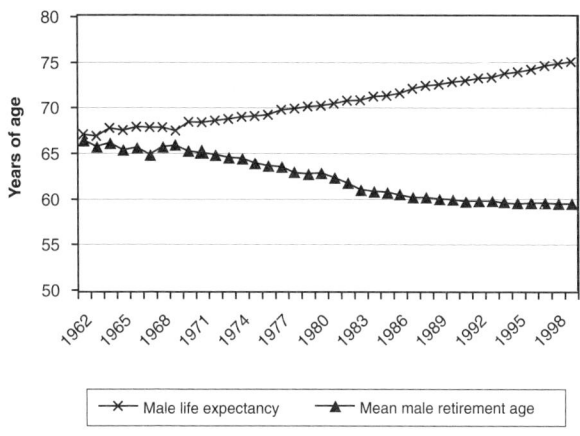

SOURCES: University of California, Berkeley and Max Planck Institute for Demographic Research, Human Mortality Database, http://www.mortality.org (accessed December 21, 2006); and Peter Scherer, *Age of Withdrawal from the Labour Force in OECD Countries* (occasional paper, Labor Market and Social Policy, OECD, Paris, France, January 11, 2002).

twenty years for men and twenty-five years for women in a number of European states (see figures 6-2 and 6-3 on the following page). And throughout Europe, this sudden radical expansion of life as a pensioner has been due not only to an increase in survival chances, but also to a retreat from the labor force—verging on a rout—on the part of older workers.

Never in history have older Europeans been so healthy, yet never, in all likelihood, have they worked so little. Figures from LABORSTA, the International Labour Office's electronic database, make the point.[2] According to those numbers, in the year 2005, barely over half of the men and women in their late fifties in Greece were economically active. In Austria in 2004, fewer than one person in eight in his or her early sixties was in the labor market. And in Denmark, the government's official labor-force

FIGURE 6-2

EXPECTED YEARS IN RETIREMENT FOR MALES, OECD COUNTRIES, 2004

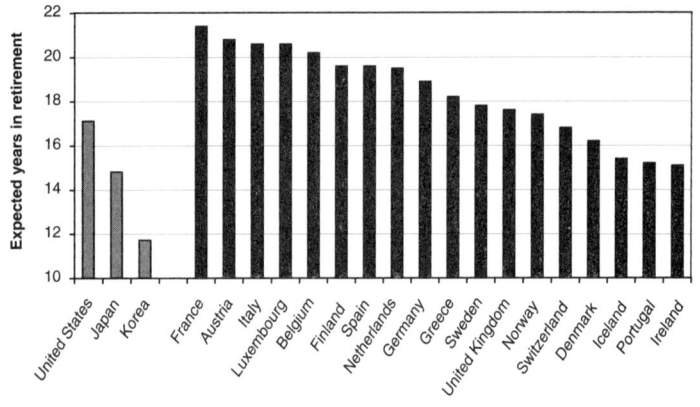

SOURCE: Organisation for Economic Co-operation and Development (OECD), *Live Longer, Work Longer 2006* (Paris: Organisation for Economic Co-operation and Development, 2006).

FIGURE 6-3

EXPECTED YEARS IN RETIREMENT FOR FEMALES, OECD COUNTRIES, 2004

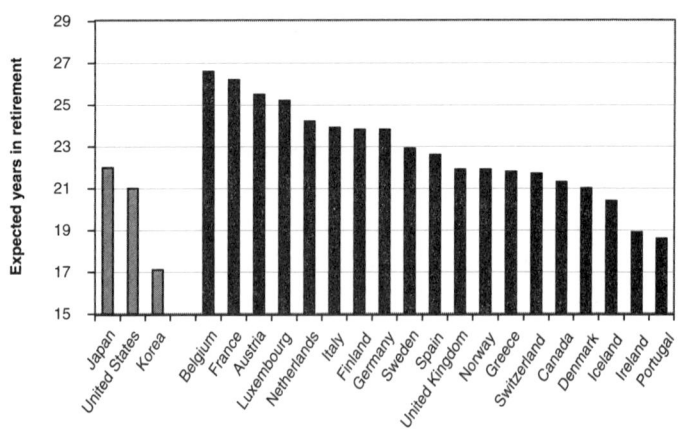

SOURCE: Organisation for Economic Co-operation and Development (OECD), *Live Longer, Work Longer 2006* (Paris: Organisation for Economic Co-operation and Development, 2006).

survey no longer even collects data on people over the age of sixty-six.

To be sure, Western Europe's current retreat from paid work at older ages is not entirely uniform, and some of the variations are both informative and potentially important (see figures 6-4 and 6-5 on the following page). One partial exception to the disposition to translate prosperity and longevity wholly into leisure, for instance, may be seen today in Switzerland. Although the Swiss enjoy one of the world's longest life expectancies, for men and women alike, the expectation of years of retired life for Swiss men and women is currently among the lowest in all of Western Europe; most unusually in Europe these days, the country's average age of retirement exceeds the official retirement age at which full pension benefits can be collected.[3] Data for the late 1990s, furthermore, indicate that over 70 percent of Swiss men and women ages fifty-five to sixty-four were economically active—a rate higher than those prevailing in either the United States or Japan.[4]

Perhaps even more noteworthy are the patterns from Western Europe's most dynamic, and fastest-growing, economies: Ireland and Iceland. Whereas the current expectation of life in retirement is four to five years higher in France than in the United States, it is two years lower in Ireland. OECD estimates, furthermore, suggest that the average retirement age for Irish men may actually have *increased* over the course of the 1980s and 1990s.[5] As for Iceland, as of 2002 a remarkable 88 percent of its men and women between the ages of fifty-five and sixty-four were economically active—a participation rate for that age group nearly twenty percentage points higher than Switzerland's and fully thirty points higher than America's.[6] According to OECD data, Iceland's effective retirement age for women is nearly sixty-eight years, and nearly seventy years for men—Europe's highest by far. OECD calculations, indeed, suggest that the Icelanders spend a higher fraction of their lives economically active than any other rich country. By this reckoning, as of 2000 an Icelandic man would be engaged in the workforce for 66 percent of his life; for an Icelandic woman, the corresponding proportion was 58 percent.[7] To put those numbers in perspective,

FIGURE 6-4
EFFECTIVE AGE OF RETIREMENT FOR MEN, 1997–2002:
WESTERN EUROPE VS. SELECTED NON-EUROPEAN OECD COUNTRIES

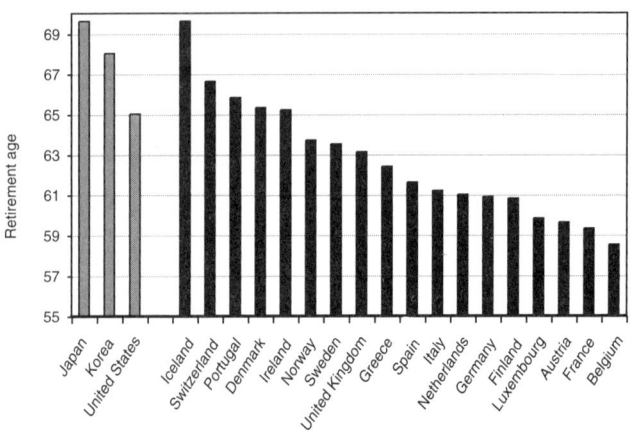

SOURCE: Organisation for Economic Co-operation and Development, *Society at a Glance: OECD Social Indicators, 2005 Edition* (Paris: OECD, 2005).

FIGURE 6-5
EFFECTIVE AGE OF RETIREMENT FOR WOMEN, 1997–2002:
WESTERN EUROPE VS. SELECTED NON-EUROPEAN OECD COUNTRIES

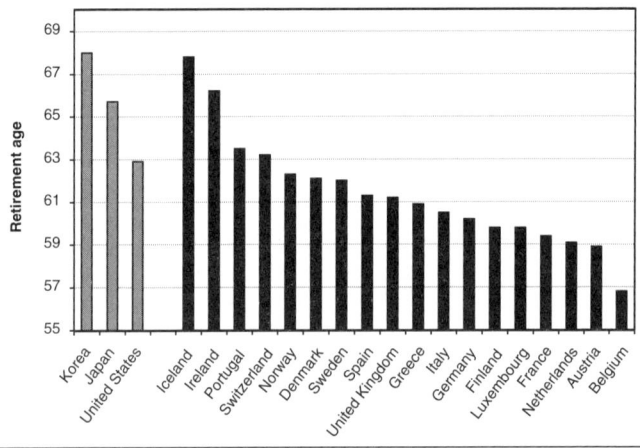

SOURCE: Organisation for Economic Co-operation and Development, *Society at a Glance: OECD Social Indicators, 2005 Edition* (Paris: OECD, 2005).

consider that men and women in Iceland devote roughly a third more of their lives to working than do their counterparts in France.[8]

Switzerland, Ireland, and Iceland may be seen as, in effect, offering nation-scale "experiments" that point to an alternative future for Europe regarding retirement arrangements. But one must also understand just how peripheral these "experimental" outliers are to the general swing of events in Europe at the moment. Taken together, these three countries have a total population of just 12 million—barely 3 percent of the Western European total. It may be that their small scale and their geographic/political status (these are either islands separated from the European mainland, or nonmembers of the EU, or, in the case of Iceland, both) facilitate a special policy flexibility; possibly other factors are at play as well. But whatever the explanation for the gap in retirement patterns between these three countries and the rest of Western Europe, we must recognize and acknowledge the overarching tendency that has for more than a generation dominated the age of withdrawal from Western European labor markets. Notwithstanding the exhortations of their politicians, or targets and timetables from their EU secretariat, the most affluent and healthy cohorts ever to inhabit Europe have, to the contrary, been choosing *en masse* to leave work behind at younger and younger ages.

The paradox of improving health but declining work is especially evident when labor-force patterns for older Europeans are contrasted with those of other affluent OECD societies (see figure 6-6 on the following page). The contrast is especially vivid when we consider the four major continental European economies: Germany, France, Italy, and Spain. Over the past generation, labor-force participation rates at older ages have gradually declined with increasing prosperity in such places as the United States, Japan, and South Korea (as might well be expected if leisure is regarded as a luxury good). Even so, a yawning gap now separates prosperous European countries from non-European counterparts. In the United States in 2004, labor-force participation rates for people in their late fifties were fully thirty percentage points higher than in Italy the following year. Labor-force participation rates for people in their early sixties were over three

FIGURE 6-6
LABOR FORCE PARTICIPATION RATES: SELECTED WESTERN
EUROPE VS. NON-EUROPEAN OECD COUNTRIES

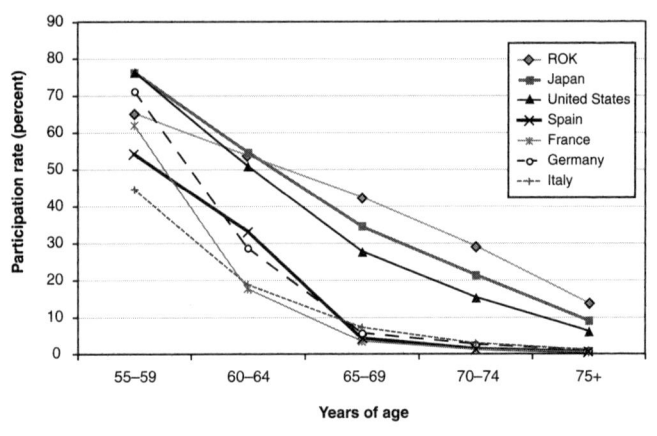

SOURCE: Source: International Labour Office, LABORSTA, http://laborsta.ilo.org/.
NOTE: Data are for 2004, except for Italy (2005).

times as high in Japan as in France—a disparity of over thirty-five percentage points—even though per-capita incomes in the two countries were roughly comparable.[9] In South Korea—whose per-capita income now exceeds that of Greece or Portugal—economic activity rates for people in their late sixties were over seven times higher than in Germany in 2004, and fully ten times higher than in Spain, making for a gap of over thirty-five points in both cases.

Europe's virtual abandonment of paid work at older ages is particularly ill-timed. As fate would have it, the *only* prospect for augmented manpower supplies in the region as a whole over the coming generation lies in the older age groups—the fifty-plus cohort. Here, a veritable manpower surge is in the making (see figure 6-7). Between the years 2005 and 2030, Western Europe's pool of younger manpower (those between the ages of fifteen and forty-nine) is projected to decline by 16 percent. On the other hand, the ranks of those fifty-five to sixty-four years of age are projected to grow by almost

FIGURE 6-7
POPULATION CHANGE IN WESTERN EUROPE VS. UNITED STATES
BY AGE GROUP, 2005–30

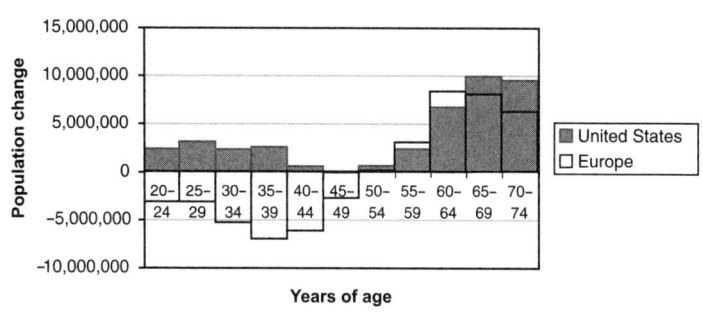

SOURCE: U.S. Census Bureau, International Data Base, http://www.census.gov/cgi-bin/ipc/idbagg (accessed May 9, 2007).

25 percent—a pace of roughly 0.9 percent per year. Western Europe's sixty-five to seventy-four cohort, for its part, is slated to swell by just under 40 percent over the next generation—a 1.5 percent annual growth tempo. In Germany the picture is somewhat different, but the bottom line is the same: While the fifteen to sixty-four age group is projected to drop by 14 percent and the fifteen to forty-nine group by 22 percent, the fifty-five to seventy-four group is expected to grow by nearly 24 percent, or over 0.9 percent per year.

If Western Europe can manage to welcome some of its older citizens back into the workforce over the coming generation—not all of them, just some!—then the region's looming incipient decline in labor supplies can not only be fully halted, but actually reversed. This currently little understood fact is absolutely central to the project of enhancing European prosperity and competitiveness in the years immediately ahead.

The stakes at play are underscored by calculations from the OECD.[10] Under current patterns of participation by age, the EU's labor force is set to shrink by about 0.2 percent per year over the three decades between 2000 and 2030. Yet if labor-force participation rates for men and women over fifty were simply to match the highest prevailing levels observed within the OECD for those same cohorts nowadays, the EU's labor force would actually *grow* over those same years by over 0.5 percent per annum, a cumulative difference of 26 percent for the entire period.[11] The magnitudes are roughly similar for Germany—a decline of about 0.4 percent per annum under present patterns, versus a yearly increase of about 0.4 percent under the alternate scenario—a net swing upward of about 0.8 percent a year, making for a workforce 27 percent larger in 2030 than would have been achieved under the contemplated "baseline."

As may be easily appreciated, an expansion of the European labor pool by 20 percent or more between now and 2030, as implied by the OECD's hardly outlandish alternative scenario for older workers' employment patterns, could have a tremendous impact on the pace of economic growth in the region over the coming generation. It is not too dramatic to suggest this could even make the difference between steady material progress and prolonged stagnation.

To be sure, some capabilities of some older workers may not match those of their youngest workmates, especially in particular types of jobs with specific sorts of demands. A recent survey of the scientific literature on age and productivity, for example, concludes that "productivity reductions at older ages [that is, after age fifty] are particularly strong for work tasks where problem solving, learning and speed are needed, while in jobs where experience and verbal abilities are important, older individuals maintain a relatively high productivity level."[12] All this may be so, and it may further be true that, as the previously mentioned Benjamin F. Jones has demonstrated, relatively few Nobel laureates do their best work after the age of fifty; but none of these arguments gainsay the potentially very substantial contributions healthy senior citizens can make to Europe's prosperity and competitiveness in the decades ahead. By translating their improved health into additional wealth, older Europeans will not just enrich themselves; they will further augment the prosperity of younger Europeans—and Europeans yet unborn.

7

Unlocking the Value of Health through New Policy: Labor Markets, Education, and Health Care

Unfortunately, there happen to be very good reasons today's older Europeans have all but fled the workforce when so many arguments would seem to militate instead for welcoming them into the ranks of the economically productive. The most obvious explanation concerns the perverse and hostile tax regimens older European would-be workers currently face. First and foremost among these are the disincentives for working at older ages currently imposed through official European tax and pension policies. In much of Western Europe, workers who elect to stay in the labor force after the age of fifty face steep financial penalties for their choice.

In Italy, the "implicit tax" on continuing to work into one's late fifties (in terms of forgone pension payments and additional pension taxes) approaches 50 percent; in France, almost 60 percent; in Belgium, it surpasses 60 percent; and in Luxembourg, it nears the astonishing level of 85 percent (see figure 7-1 on the following page). Not surprisingly, the attendant drop-off in labor-force participation rates is sharp. In Luxembourg, at what should be near-peak working ages, the labor-force participation rate for fifty-five- to fifty-nine-year-olds stands at less than 47 percent. By contrast, in the United States and Japan, where such "implicit taxes" on continued work are minimal, the drop-off between the early fifties and late fifties is also minimal—and the rates of economic activity for people in their late fifties are almost thirty percentage points higher than in Luxembourg.

Ending Europe's perverse official discouragement of work at older ages is an obvious and necessary step to unlocking the value

41

FIGURE 7-1

INCENTIVES TO RETIRE AND RETIREMENT BEHAVIOR: FALL IN MALE LABOR
FORCE PARTICIPATION BETWEEN AGES 50–54 AND 55–59

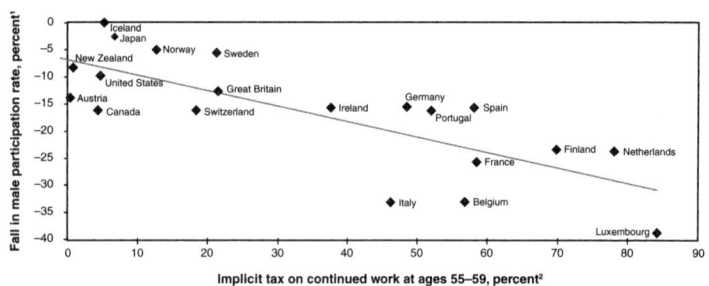

SOURCE: Figure and text from Geir H. Haarde, "Strengthening Growth and Public Finances in an Era of Demographic Change" (Background Paper, Organisation for Economic Co-operation and Development, Paris, France, May 13–14, 2004). Original data from Romain Duval, "The Retirement Effects of Old-Age Pension and Early Retirement Schemes in OECD Countries" (Working Paper 370, Organisation for Economic Co-operation and Development, Economics Department, Paris, France, November 2003).

NOTES: 1. Difference in participation rates between the age groups 55–59 and 50–54 as a percentage of the participation rate of those ages 50–54 years.

2. The implicit tax on working an additional year is the forgone transfer/pension income plus the additional pension contributions paid, minus any increase in future pensions as a result of delayed retirement, all expressed as a share of income from work. The calculations in all cases take account of the "regular" old-age pension scheme but consider somewhat different early retirement pathways depending on the country in question or, where such schemes do not apply widely, no such pathways.

of health over the coming generation for the peoples of the region. Yet restoring tax neutrality in this area is but a single step on a much longer and more comprehensive path. Making much fuller economic use of Europe's comparative advantage in health will require nothing less than a fundamental reexamination of many of the basic policies and arrangements currently taken for granted in Western European daily life.

We do not propose any detailed plans or long-range programs here. The precursor to any such manifestos must be an intellectual groundwork, derived from a far-reaching, open-minded, and unflinching public conversation about what is working well in the current European approaches to "healthy aging"—and also about what should be working very much better. In the spirit of constructive criticism, we will simply mention three facets of social and economic life where such a rethinking of existing European policies and arrangements seems particularly pressing: labor markets, education, and health policy.

Labor Markets

The structural problems of contemporary European labor markets are not exactly an international secret. By any global measure, European economies are characterized by strikingly high levels of unemployment and remarkably long spells of idleness for those who are unemployed. Whereas, for example, fewer than 10 percent of Canada's unemployed had been out of work for over one year as of 2005, the corresponding figure among the jobless in the EU-15 was nearly 44 percent.[1] These rigidities, however, have been imposed on Europe's job markets more or less by deliberate design; they directly reflect official employment policies, regulations, and restrictions.

The consequence of these distortions has been the emergence over the past generation of the "underworked European," a phenomenon vividly illustrated in figure 7-2 on the following page. Not only are Europe's labor-force participation rates lower—and often sharply lower—than those of non-European OECD countries, but the hours worked by those actually employed have dropped precipitously in recent decades. At this point, in fact, the typical Italian employee works two hundred fewer hours per year than his or her American counterpart. For French and German workers, the corresponding gap is almost four hundred hours per year—the equivalent of roughly one workday every week! This U.S.-Europe work gap has materialized despite a drop of roughly 10 percent in annual hours per employee in America itself between the early 1960s and the start of the twenty-first century.

Western Europe's remarkably low availability of work (the flipside of its remarkably low rates of labor utilization) cannot be explained

FIGURE 7-2
ANNUAL HOURS WORKED: UNITED STATES VS. MAJOR
CONTINENTAL ECONOMIES

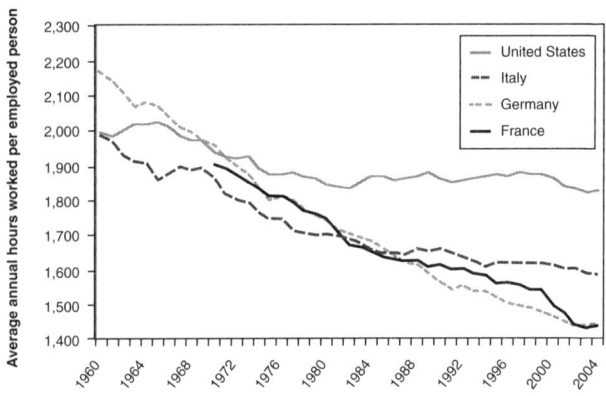

SOURCE: Graphic originally from Alberto Alesina, Edward Glaeser, and Bruce Sacerdote, "Work and Leisure in the U.S. and Europe: Why So Different?" (Discussion Paper 2068, Harvard Institute of Economic Research, Cambridge, Mass., April 2005), figure 1. Reconstructed using Source OECD, Employment and Labour Market Statistics, http://www.sourceoecd.org (accessed July 27, 2007).
NOTE: Pre-1991 values for Germany are West Germany only. OECD statistical sources caution that "the[se] data are intended for comparisons of trends over time."

away as a consequence of affluence or "special European tastes for leisure."[2] To the contrary, today's "underworked European" is primarily a creation of the policy environment. By and large, for example, Western European countries have made it expensive to hire, and difficult to fire, new workers. Consequently, European employers tend to be exceptionally cautious about taking on new hires.

For would-be older workers, the climate is especially difficult, since customary seniority rules often mean that elders are awarded benefit packages in excess of their individual productivity—a practice that transforms older prospective employees into undesirable profit-killers for any competitive enterprise. Further, by a sort of zero-sum thinking no less prevalent for its manifest illogic, many

Europeans believe that any job offered to an older worker is one taken away from someone younger—as if there were some fixed and unchanging job total available for the continent, so that one person's gain must be another's loss.

It is certainly true that the job market for young people in Europe has been neither vibrant nor especially promising for quite some time. It is an environment that discourages young Europeans from seeking work in the first place, with those who do knowing that unemployment rates tend to be the very highest for their age group.[3] But young men and women in Europe are not being frozen out of the workforce by their elders, much less senior citizens. Rather, young and old Europeans alike commonly are suffering from economic regimens that artificially depress the demand for their labor. Redressing the "lose-lose" dysfunctions in Europe's labor markets will generate more wealth, more consumer and business demand, and more job opportunities for all—irrespective of the age of the given worker.

If Europe hopes to gain economic benefit from its looming surge in prospective older workers, its labor markets must be far more flexible, and more economically rational, than they are today. And lest it go unsaid: As part of this reworking, some orderly transition to a system of pension funding that entails a greater measure of direct personal responsibility in the financing of retirement would also seem to be entirely in order.[4]

Education

Although the future promises to produce the best-trained cohort of senior workers that Europe has ever seen, skills and training in a rapidly changing, knowledge-based economy cannot be allowed to remain stagnant. While some spontaneous on-the-job training will always take place, a more deliberate strategy for constantly upgrading the capabilities of all workers, including older ones, would be welcome. At the moment, "lifelong learning" is a slogan in Europe, not a practice; enormous differences can be seen among countries in both the regularity and the quality of supplemental on-the-job training or education.[5] To support real lifelong education, Europe will need a systematic shift—not just in policies, but in underlying culture.

Without belaboring the issue, two additional observations about "lifelong learning" may be apposite here. First, as Nobel laureate in economics James J. Heckman has observed, "Skill begets skill and learning begets learning."[6] In other words, "lifelong education" should properly commence at the *start* of life. Yet, by many indications, there is considerable room for improvement in the education and training of Europe's rising generations. As table 3-1 on page 17 underscored, the continent today is home not only to the "underworked European," but also to the "undereducated European"—and very often these turn out to be one and the same person.[7]

This leads us to a second point: Skill acquisition and augmentation requires reinforcement through work. Heckman stressed this point in a recent survey of the European scene, saying that "Europe's skill utilization is low" and "the maintenance of human capital is [also] worrisome." "Skill formation is impaired," he explained, "when returns to skill formation are low due to low skill use and insufficient skill maintenance later in life." In particular, he suggested that "Europe's future problems with low skills" are "exacerbated by labor market institutions and government policies that lower utilization rates of human capital and promote steep depreciation of human capital over the life cycle." Thus, in Heckman's view, European policies today are not only creating human capital but destroying it. To promote "lifelong education" successfully, he advises that "policies to foster human capital cannot be seen in isolation from labor market policies, tax and benefit systems and pension schemes."[8]

Health-Care Policy

Then there is the hardly trivial question of health-care policy. Medical and health services already absorb a very substantial share of total expenditures in the modern European economies. With pronounced population aging, among other "drivers," those outlays promise to rise in the years ahead, possibly even more rapidly than in the recent past. By the same token, the share of national resources absorbed by the health and medical sectors stands only to grow over the coming decades. There is widespread apprehension throughout Europe today about the specter of explosive, unmanageable health-care costs in the era ahead.

We would respectfully suggest that most of this health-cost "angst" is, in essence, misplaced. After all, in an economic development regimen powered primarily by human resources and human capital, the cost of medical care must be assessed in terms of the value of health. Viewed a little less emotionally and a little more pragmatically, the medical sector and the life-science industries should be seen as part of the critical supporting structure under-girding an increasingly health-dependent—and health-intensive—modern economy that needs, particularly in Europe, longer and more sustainable phases of work-life productivity in order to compete successfully against other regions.

Although contemporary political discourse often proceeds as if medical and health-care expenditures were nothing more than a huge cost imposed upon modern industrial economies, the plain fact is that health and medical services *augment* the wealth of societies and the citizens therein. Few of us seem to appreciate the truly monumental scale of this contribution. Kevin M. Murphy and Robert H. Topel, for example, have estimated that the economic value of the mortality reductions and health improvements enjoyed by the American population over the years 1970–2000 amounted to roughly $60 trillion.[9] That estimate, we should emphasize, is for the net value of health improvements after health and medical expenditures have been factored out. Analogous research for Europe would underscore the immense economic benefits that currently accrue from health services on the other side of the Atlantic.

To capitalize upon its edge in health, Europe must continue to invest in health. Allocations to the health and medical sectors should be regarded in the main as investments.[10] Do we worry because fixed investment in machinery and equipment accounts for a much higher percentage of national output today than a century ago?[11] Bear in mind, furthermore, that research and innovation can provide improved quality at lower cost in the medical realm, just as they do in other economic sectors.[12] Research plays a critical role here—and there is evidence that affluent societies may be spending far too little, rather than far too much, on innovation in this realm. One recent important study on health research needs in the United States, for example, concluded that, from the standpoint of economic returns, the optimal level of public funding for biomedical and life sciences research for America would be roughly three or four times higher than actual current allocations.[13] Given Europe's relatively low overall levels of investment in research and development in comparison with Japan and the United States,[14] it would not be surprising if the gap between actual and optimal investment in biomedical research were even greater for Western Europe today.

To be clear: Our perspective on health affairs does not—indeed cannot—justify any specific health-care policy, medical-service price, or life-sciences project *a priori*. As in all other economic sectors, the cost of any particular measure in the health field might well be unjustified or unwarranted; any particular proposed outlay or initiative might not withstand cost-benefit scrutiny. But with the new economic opportunities arising from "healthy aging" in Europe, the rates of return on future investments in health could be very high indeed in future years. In the nineteenth century, the great physician and epidemiologist Rudolf Karl Virchow declared,

> Wenn die Medizin ihre grosse Aufgabe erfüllen soll, muss sie in das politische und soziale Leben einfliessen. (If medicine is really to accomplish its great task, it must intervene in political and social life.)[15]

At the dawn of the twenty-first century, we must also include medicine's potentially tremendous impact on economic life as one of its great assignments. And if European health policy shifts focus from containing the cost of medical expenditures to minimizing the cost of illness and disease, it will be that much better poised to fulfill this assignment.[16]

Concluding Remarks

A generation from now, will Europe be steadily losing ground to emerging competitors, resigned to its status as a follower economy? Or will it retain its current ranking as a top-prosperity locale that is home to many cutting-edge, globally competitive industries? It is true that Europe's demographic pressures are heavy, and, without creative response, they will weigh increasingly toward that first vision of the future. If Europe does not rise to its demographic challenges, furthermore, the continent can probably enjoy the equivalent of a prolonged and comfortable (albeit ever more modest) retirement. But relative economic decline is by no means inevitable for Europe or its people.

Despite population aging and demographic stagnation, Europe need not become a glorious rest home or a genteel, but increasingly shabby, open-air museum. There is another way—and the choice of which way to go belongs to Europeans themselves.

Notes

Chapter 1: The Demographic Challenge to European Prosperity

1. In the interest of clarity, we should begin by defining just what we mean by "Europe" in the following pages. While some may believe the demarcations and geographical boundaries of "Europe" are obvious and self-evident, they do not always match up when one observer's "Europe" is compared with another's. In truth, the common understanding of exactly what territories comprise "Europe" has been a sort of work-in-progress for the past 2,500 years (before which time "Europe" really only referred to the mainland areas of classical Greece).

In our discussion, "Europe" is shorthand for the more affluent, never-Communist, territories and societies within the greater European expanse—that is to say, the region that was commonly called "Western Europe" during the Cold War era. We fully recognize the empirical limitations of this definition, excluding as it does over 300 million of the 700 million people that the United Nations (among others) currently counts as "Europeans." But if this is a conceit, it is not our own—to the contrary, it is one shared by the governments of the territories in question and increasingly, it would seem, by the citizens in question as well. With the end of the Cold War, many who would once have described themselves as "Western European" have come to identify themselves simply as "European"—a shift, one may note, that is very much in consonance with the aims of the greater political project now known as the European Union.

For the purist, our definition of "Europe"/"Western Europe" as the never-Communist areas of the European landmass is not without provisos and exceptions. Germany, for example, is very much part of the "Europe" we will be discussing, even though the "New Federal States" of reunified Germany were part of the Warsaw Pact until 1990. Austria is also very much a part of Western Europe, despite eastern Austria's having been the "Soviet Zone" of the postwar Allied Occupation for a full decade, from 1945 to 1955.

By the same token, today's commonly used official terminologies—which will be used frequently here—offer varying approximations of what we mean by "Europe," some of them closer approximations than others. "EU-15" includes the fifteen member states of the "European Union" as of May 1, 2004: Austria, Belgium, Denmark, Finland, France, Germany, Greece, Ireland, Italy, Luxembourg, the Netherlands, Portugal, Spain, Sweden, and the United Kingdom. "OECD Europe" comprises all the European states admitted to the Organization for Economic Cooperation and Development as of this writing (2007)—that is to say, the EU-15 plus three Western European non-EU members (Iceland, Norway, and Switzerland) and four states from the former Warsaw Pact (the Czech Republic, Hungary, Poland, and the Slovak Republic). "Western Europe," as informally defined by the United States Bureau of the Census, includes eighteen of the twenty-two countries of OECD Europe (all but the Czech Republic, Hungary, Poland, and the Slovak Republic), plus the tiny populations of nine additional islands, royal territories, or republics situated west of the Danube.

In our discussion, we use "EU-15" and "the eighteen states of Western Europe" (EU-15, plus Iceland, Norway, and Switzerland) as proxies for Western Europe as a whole. In practical terms, these are both very close approximations. As of midyear 2005, the population of "Western Europe," according to U.S. Census Bureau estimates, numbered 397.8 million persons. The EU-15 group accounted for an estimated 384.6 million—amounting to almost 97 percent of the total for Western Europe. The eighteen states of Western Europe, for their part, contained an estimated 397.0 million inhabitants, a coverage rate of 99.8 percent. Only about 13 million people in all of Western Europe lived outside the EU-15—and fewer than a million lived outside of the region's eighteen major states.

2. Derived from OECD data, based on GDP at constant 2000 price levels and exchange rates; SourceOECD, National Accounts Statistics, http://www.sourceoecd.org (accessed August 30, 2006).

Chapter 2: U.S.-European Demographic Divergence

1. Note that we use projections from the U.S. Census Bureau in our following discussion. Our analysis, however, is not sensitive to the source of these projections, since projections by other authoritative organizations—including EUROSTAT, UN Population Division, Statistisches Bundesamt, and others—offer broadly similar assessments and scenarios for the countries and regions under consideration here. More specifically, the Census Bureau projections utilized here come from its International Data Base

(IDB), which is maintained by the Census Bureau's International Programs Center and available at http://www.census.gov/ipc/www/idb/ (accessed August 16, 2007). IDB projections undergo continuous updating and revision; our analysis draws upon projections as of June 1, 2007.

2. Benjamin F. Jones, "Age and Great Invention" (Working Paper 11359, National Bureau of Economic Research, May 2005), http://www.nber.org/papers/11359 (accessed July 2, 2007).

3. Some recent research suggests the age composition of the labor-force may, indeed, have a more than incidental influence on productivity and innovation. James Feyrer, for example, has argued that workers in their forties seem to make a special contribution to growth in modern economies. He attributes part of the growth acceleration in the United States in the 1990s to its surge of forty-somethings and, conversely, attributes part of Japan's poor economic performance in recent decades to the country's sharp drop-off in workers in their forties; see James Feyrer, "Demographics and Productivity," *Review of Economics and Statistics* 89, no. 1 (January 2007): 100–109.

4. IDB population projections for most countries and regions start in the mid-1990s and extend to 2050. For demographic estimates for years not covered by the IDB, we rely in this analysis upon United Nations Population Division, World Population Prospects: The 2006 Revision Population Database, http://esa.un.org/unpp (for medium variant population; accessed June 1, 2007).

Chapter 3: Europe's Limited Demographic Options

1. U.S. Census Bureau, International Data Base, http://www.census.gov/ipc/www/idbnew.html (for total midyear population; accessed August 16, 2007); United Nations Population Division, World Population Prospects.

2. Giampaolo Lanzieri, "Population in Europe 2005: First Results," *Statistics in Focus* 16 (November 2006), http://epp.eurostat.ec.europa.eu/cache/ITY_OFFPUB/KS-NK-06-016/EN/KS-NK-06-016-EN.PDF (accessed July 2, 2007).

3. Here we draw upon Eurostat projections for the EU-15, rather than "Western Europe" as defined by the U.S. Census Bureau—but since the population of the EU-15 accounts for approximately 97 percent of the total population of "Western Europe," the crossover point should be very close for the two entities. Eurostat projections for EU-15 are from Eurostat, Population Data, http://epp.eurostat.ec.europa.eu/portal/page?_pageid=1996, 45323734&_dad=portal&_schema=PORTAL&screen=welcomeref&open=/

popula/proj/proj_trend&language=en&product=EU_MASTER_population
&root=EU_MASTER_population&scrollto=0 (accessed May 9, 2007).

4. As indeed they are. Lacking as they do any biological referents, the demographic projections for migration flows are especially open to question. For a serious but severe assessment of the state of migration projections concerning Western Europe, see Xavier Thierry, "Avenir des migrations européennes: Regard critique sur les projections des Nations Unies," *Agir* (Paris) 29 (January 2007): 54–62.

5. Institut National de la Statistique et des Études Économiques, "Le bilan démographique 2006—un exédent naturel record," January 16, 2007, http://www.insee.fr/fr/ffc/pop_age4.htm (accessed May 9, 2007).

6. Conventionally, demographers use a TFR of 2.1 as a notional shorthand for the birth level required for population replacement. In reality, the requisite TFR may be either slightly below this benchmark or well above it, depending on mortality patterns for children and young adults and, thus, the survival schedules for the successive generation rising to childbearing ages.

7. This outlook, we hasten to add, should not be dismissed as simply French chauvinism. As France's leading demographers and social historians have underscored, there has indeed been something highly unusual about the country's demographic rhythms—not just recently, but over the *longue durée*. France, after all, was the first country in Europe—indeed, in the world—to enter into sustained fertility decline through deliberate limitation of family size—embarking upon this process nearly a century before the rest of Europe and, indeed, before industrialization had made significant inroads into social life. By the same token, population growth in France has been uniquely slow among countries in the now developed regions. See, for example, Jean Bourgeois-Pichat, "Évolution générale de la population française depuis le XVIIe siècle," *Population* 6, no. 4 (1951): 635–62; and Fernand Braudel, *L'Identité de France,* vol. 1, (Paris: Arthaud-Flammarion, 1986), 165–200. It should hardly surprise that French writers and thinkers are equally disposed to regard their nation's current demographic patterns as exceptional.

8. "France seems to escape by some miracle from the 'European demographic winter,' thanks to its fertility rate of 1.9 children per woman. Is the French exception . . . viable over the long run?" Nicolas Sarkozy, "Démographie et politique," *Agir* 29 (January 2007): 16.

9. David Coleman, "Immigration and Ethnic Change in Low-Fertility Countries: A Third Demographic Transition," *Population and Development Review* 32, no. 3 (September 2006): 401–46.

10. Eurostat, *Population Statistics: 2006 Edition* (Luxembourg: Eurostat, 2006), tables D-4, D-6.

11. For estimates of various measures of U.S. fertility for the 1960–2002 period, see Brady E. Hamilton, "Reproduction Rates for 1990–2002 and Intrinsic Rates for 2000–2001: United States," *National Vital Statistics Reports* 52, no. 17 (March 18, 2004), http://www.cdc.gov/nchs/data/nvsr/nvsr52/nvsr 52_17.pdf (accessed May 31, 2007).

12. Eurostat, *Population Statistics*, tables G-5, G-11. We are obliged to note that, formally, there was no EU-15 in 1975; the fifteenth European member of the EU did not join that collectivity until twenty years later, in 1995. But we trust readers will understand what we mean here.

13. Council of Europe, *Recent Demographic Developments in Europe 2005* (Strasbourg: Council of Europe, 2006), tables T2.1, T2.3.

14. Guy Laroque and Bernard Salinie, "Does Fertility Respond to Financial Incentives?" (Discussion Paper 5007, Center for Economic Policy Research, London, April 2005).

15. This discussion uses Eurostat's "no migration" projection scenario (which posits zero net migration into the EU-15 from 2004 onward) in comparison with its "baseline" population projection. Although there are some differences between Eurostat and Census Bureau projection series, the projected impact of zero net immigration for Western Europe and the EU-15 would be much the same in either series.

16. Giampaolo Lanzieri and Veronica Corsini, "First Demographic Estimates for Europe 2005," *Statistics in Focus* 1 (January 2006), http://epp.eurostat.ec .europa.eu/cache/ITY_OFFPUB/KS-NK-06-001/EN/KS-NK-06-001-EN.PDF (accessed July 2, 2007).

17. Eurostat, *Population Statistics*, tables F-3, F-5, F-7.

18. We realize that international comparisons of educational attainment beg the question of comparability of training—whether, for example, a high school diploma from the United States is fully equivalent to one from France or Greece. Such questions, however, are largely circumvented in this comparison, since presumably most of the émigrés residing in the United States were educated in the schooling system of their own native lands.

19. For the purposes of standardizing international comparisons, we use here the definition of "tertiary education" currently offered in the International Standard Classification of Education (ISCED-97) and embraced by the OECD in its compilations of international educational statistics. For the U.S. educational system, "tertiary education" would include not only graduate study and a bachelor's degree from college, but also training for a college associate's degree. See United Nations Educational, Scientific and Cultural Organization (UNESCO), *International Standard Classification of Education: ISCED 1997*, 34–38, http://www.uis. unesco.org/TEMPLATE/pdf/isced/ISCED_A.pdf (accessed July 3, 2007).

20. For one thing, the educational data for Western Europeans pertain to adults no older than sixty-four, while the figures on Western Europeans in the United States include the population sixty-five years and older—a cohort whose educational attainment is likely to be lower than that of the twenty-five-to sixty-four-year-old group. For another, the pool of Western Europeans living in the United States today includes many who moved there several decades earlier—at a time when educational attainment on both sides of the Atlantic was lower than it is today. As of the 2000 census, for example, roughly half of all European-born inhabitants of the United States had moved to America before 1980—that is to say, over twenty years before the 2000 census "snapshot" of adult educational profiles was taken. Given the "stock-flow" nature of the immigration dynamic, and the progressively rising levels of education in all OECD societies, we might expect the educational profile of the newest immigrants from Western Europe to be progressively increasing as well. One possible counterbalancing factor, which might tend to overstate the apparent educational differentials in table 3-1 between Western Europeans who migrate and those who do not, might be the U.S. predisposition to continue training throughout the working ages. If the U.S. social and economic environment supports (or rewards) continuing training more than the European business environment does, the reported educational differentials in table 3-1 between native and émigré Western Europeans could, in part, reflect additional training that immigrants had acquired after arriving in the United States—thereby exaggerating the educational differences between migrators and nonmigrators at the actual time of migration. Without further empirical research, we cannot determine the actual educational profiles of the most recent arrivals to the United States from Western Europe—but, taken together, the qualifications and considerations just outlined would seem to weigh in favor of the proposition that the current differentials may be even wider than the ones reported in table 3-1.

21. Estimates from U.S. Census Bureau, "United States Foreign-Born Population," http://www.census.gov/population/www/socdemo/foreigndatatbls. html (accessed February 21, 2007).

22. Hendrik P. van Dalen and Kene Henkens, "Longing for the Good Life: Understanding Emigration from a High-Income Country," *Population and Development Review* 33, no. 1 (March 2007): 37–65.

23. Michèle Tribalat, "Vers un sélectivité et un contrôle accrus des politiques migratoires en Europe," *Agir* (Paris) 29 (January 2007): 39.

Chapter 4: Healthy Aging

1. Low mortality is not identical to "good health." In some cases, low-mortality populations suffer from a high burden of disease and illness (for example, Cuba, rural China, and Sri Lanka), and, conversely we can think of instances of robust populations with very high death rates (wartime infantry forces, for example). Yet, on the whole and under ordinary circumstances, mortality levels happen to be a very good proxy for general health level—and general mortality levels, furthermore, correspond quite closely with a population's economic potential.

2. Cf. Lant H. Pritchett and Lawrence H. Summers, "Wealthier Is Healthier," *Journal of Human Resources* 31, no. 4 (Autumn 1996): 841–68; Robert W. Fogel, "Health, Nutrition and Economic Growth," *Economic Development and Cultural Change* 52, no. 3 (April 2004): 643–58; and T. Paul Schultz, "Human Capital and Development," in *Agricultural Competitiveness*, ed. G. H. Peters et al. (Aldershot, England: Dartmouth Publishing Group, 1995). For additional perspectives on the impact of the interplay of health and wealth on human welfare, see Gary S. Becker, Tomas J. Philipson, and Rodrigo R. Soares, "The Quantity and Quality of Life and the Evolution of World Inequality" (Working Paper 9765, National Bureau of Economic Research, Cambridge, Mass., 2003).

3. Elizabeth Arias, "United States Life Table, 2003," *National Vital Statistics Reports* 54, no. 14 (April 19, 2006), http://www.cdc.gov/nchs/data/nvsr/nvsr 54/nvsr54_14.pdf (accessed May 9, 2007).

4. Eurostat, *Population Statistics*, tables E-4, E-5.

5. This is to say that, all else being equal, the "net present value" of education will be higher in a setting where health is better and mortality rates are lower.

6. See Dora L. Costa, "Understanding the Twentieth-Century Decline in Chronic Conditions among Older Men," *Demography* 37, no. 1 (February 2000): 53–72; Costa, "Changing Chronic Disease Rates and Long-Term Declines in Functional Limitation among Older Men," *Demography* 39, no.1 (February 2002): 119–37; Robert W. Fogel, "Changes in the Disparities in Chronic Diseases during the Course of the Twentieth Century" (Working Paper 10311, National Bureau of Economic Research, February 2004); and Fogel, *The Escape from Hunger and Premature Death, 1700–2100* (New York: Cambridge University Press, 2004).

7. Robert W. Fogel, "Secular Trends in Physiological Capital: Implications for Equity in Health Care" (Working Paper 9771, National Bureau of Economic Research, June 2003).

8. Uta Ziegler and Gabriela Dolbhammer, "Steigende Lebenserwartung geht mit besserer Gesundheit einher: Risiko der Pflegebedürftigkeit in

Deutschland sinkt," *Demografische Forschung aus Erster Hand* 2, no. 1 (January 2005), http://www.demografische-forschung.org/archiv/defo0501.pdf (accessed July 2, 2007).

9. James Oeppen and James W. Vaupel, "Broken Limits to Life Expectancy," *Science* 296, no. 5570 (May 10, 2002): 1029–31

10. James W. Vaupel et al., "Biodemographic Trajectories of Longevity," *Science* 280, no. 5365 (May 8, 1998): 855–60.

11. Roland Rau, Eugeny Soroko, Domantas Jasilionis, and James W. Vaupel, "Ten Years after Kannisto: Further Evidence for Mortality Decline at Advanced Ages in Developed Countries" (Working Paper 2006-033, Max Planck Institute for Demographic Research, October 2006).

12. Beth J. Soldo, Olivia S. Mitchell, Rania Tfaily, and John F. McCabe, "Cross-Cohort Differences in Health on the Verge of Retirement" (Working Paper 12762, National Bureau of Economic Research, December 2006).

13. Each of the cycles of the Retirement and Health Survey upon which this analysis was based included just over 5,000 respondents, as cited by Soldo et. al.

14. Oeppen and Vaupel, "Broken Limits to Life Expectancy."

Chapter 5: Enhancing Prosperity through Healthy Aging

1. For a thought-provoking assessment of the potentialities for employment at older ages in Europe in the decades ahead, see James W. Vaupel and Elke Loichinger, "Redistributing Work in Aging Europe," *Science* 312, no. 5782 (June 30, 2006): 1911–13. Note, however, that Vaupel and Loichinger are largely describing the possibility of *redistributing* work over the lifecycle. From our perspective, the economic opportunities of "healthy aging" lie not just in redistributing productive work, but also in augmenting it.

Chapter 6: Europe's Ongoing Retreat from the Workplace

1. Organisation for Economic Co-operation and Development (OECD), *Live Longer, Work Longer* (Paris: OECD, 2006), 33.

2. International Labour Office, LABORSTA Internet, http://laborsta.ilo.org (accessed July 2, 2007).

3. OECD, *Live Longer, Work Longer*, 32–33.

4. David Dorn and Alfonso Sousa-Poza, "Why is the Employment Rate of Older Swiss So High? An Analysis of the Social Security System," *European Papers on the New Welfare*, no. 1 (2005), http://eng.newwelfare.org/?p=188&page=1 (accessed July 2, 2007). On the other hand, Switzerland is hardly untouched by the temptations for early retirement evident on the rest

of the continent, or the stratagems for seizing a lucrative early pension. Thus, as the health of the Swiss population continues to improve, so does the number of early retirees claiming "health problems" as their justification for drawing an early pension. See Jean-François Rudaz, "Einfluss des Gesundheitszustandes auf den Altersrücktritt," *Die Volkswirtschaft* (Bern), no. 10 (2005), http://www.smd.ch/faksimile/f200510/vow_20051001_1005 _1_1.pdf (accessed May 31, 2007).

5. Jean-Marc Burniaux, Romain Duval, and Florence Jaumotte, "Coping with Ageing: A Dynamic Approach to Quantify the Impact of Alternative Policy Options on Future Labor Supply in OECD Countries" (Working Paper no. 371, OECD Economics Department, 2004).

6. International Labour Office, LABORSTA Internet.

7. Burniaux et al., "Coping with Ageing," 86.

8. The contraposition is all the more meaningful when one considers that Iceland's educational profile and its per-capita income level are both slightly higher than France's. For the educational profiles, see table 3-1; for national level of per-capita output, see Organisation for Economic Co-operation and Development, "GDP Per Capita, USP, Converted Using PPPs, 2003," http://ocde.p4.siteinternet.com/publications/doifiles/ 012004071B0G002.xls (accessed June 15, 2007).

9. According to the OECD, GDP per capita (with purchasing power parity [PPP] adjustments) was slightly higher in Japan than in France in 2003; see Organisation for Economic Co-operation and Development, "GDP Per Capita." On the other hand, according to the eminent economic historian Angus Maddison, per-capita GDP (adjusted for purchasing power) was slightly higher in France than in Japan as of 2003; see Angus Maddison, "World Population, GDP and GDP Per Capita, 1–2003 AD," http:// www.ggdc.net/maddison/Historical_Statistics/horizontal-file_03-2007.xls (accessed June 15, 2007). Taken together, these estimates emphasize the basic comparability of per-capita output levels in Japan and France at the start of the new century.

10. Mark Keese, "Ageing and Employment in Europe: A Summary of OECD Evidence and Perspectives" (report, Organisation for Economic Co-operation and Development and International Longevity Center, Paris, April 2005), http://www.ilc-france.org/actualites/docs/OECDpaper_22April.pdf (accessed May 9, 2007).

11. The OECD's alternative scenario, incidentally, is not terribly radical. First, it explicitly excludes "outlier" countries like Mexico and Turkey from consideration. Second, today's "highest" participation rates for men are generally lower than they were in the same "high" countries just a generation

ago. Finally, while today's "highest" rates for older women are typically higher than a generation ago, they are still considerably lower than for older men these days.

12. Vigard Skirbegg, "Age and Individual Productivity: A Literature Survey" (Working Paper WP-2003-028, Max Planck Institute for Demographic Research, August 2003), http://www.demogr.mpg.de/ papers/working/wp-2003-028.pdf (accessed May 9, 2007).

Chapter 7: Unlocking the Value of Health through New Policy

1. Organisation for Economic Co-operation and Development, *Labour Force Statistics 1985–2005* (Paris: OECD, 2006), 47.

2. For a detailed and persuasive refutation of such presumptions, see Alberto Alesina, Edward Glaeser, and Bruce Sacerdote, "Work and Leisure in the U.S. and Europe: Why So Different?" (Discussion Paper 2068, Harvard Institute of Economic Research, April 2005), http://econweb.fas. harvard.edu/hier/2005papers/HIER2068.pdf (accessed June 1, 2007).

3. The situation can be underscored by a single, admittedly extreme, exemplary comparison: Whereas in 2005 roughly 44 percent of Americans ages sixteen to nineteen and 75 percent of those twenty to twenty-four were economically active, the corresponding proportions for Italians ages fifteen to nineteen and twenty to twenty-four were 14 percent and 53 percent, respectively—a gap of well over twenty percentage points! (International Labour Office, LABORSTA Internet). The disparity, incidentally, cannot be explained in terms of educational enrollment or attainment profiles. As of 2001, attainment levels were almost thirty percentage points lower for both tertiary and upper secondary education among Italians ages twenty-five to thirty-four than among their U.S. counterparts. Cf. Organisation for Economic Co-operation and Development, *Education at a Glance: OECD Indicators, 2002* (Paris: OECD, 2002), charts A1.2 and A2.3.

4. For some perspectives on undoing Western Europe's current labor market distortions, see Martin Neil Baily and Jacob Funk Kierkegaard, *Transforming the European Economy* (Washington, D.C.: Institute for International Economics, 2004); André Sapir, Philippe Aghion, Giuseppe Bertola, Martin Hellwig, Jean Pisani-Ferry, Dariusz Rosati, José Viñals, and Helen Wallace, *An Agenda for a Growing Europe: The Sapir Report* (New York: Oxford University Press, 2004); and Alberto Alesina and Francesco Giavazzi, *The Future of Europe: Reform or Decline* (Cambridge, Mass.: MIT Press, 2006).

5. For more information on this point, see Organisation for Economic Co-operation and Development, *Live Longer, Work Longer*, chapter 6, and Keese, "Ageing and Employment in Europe," 18–20.

6. James J. Heckman and Bas Jacobs, "Policies to Create and Destroy Human Capital in Europe," in *Perspectives on the Performance of the Continent's Economies*, ed. Hans-Werner Sinn and Edmund Phelps (Cambridge, Mass.: MIT Press, forthcoming).

7. Note that we do not contend that the quality of education is entirely comparable between European countries and the United States (or, for that matter, from one European country to the next). The metric of educational attainment (years completed in the educational system) offers only a crude proxy for the actual skills and training imparted through schooling. Imperfect though this approximation may be, it nevertheless provides a useful—and meaningful—starting point for analysis here.

8. Heckman and Jacobs, "Policies to Create and Destroy Human Capital."

9. Kevin M. Murphy and Robert H. Topel, "The Value of Health and Longevity," *Journal of Political Economy* 114, no. 5 (October 2006): 871–904.

10. But we should never forget that health is not only an investment good but also a consumption good—or, to put it another way, it is a factor that generates not only positive productive returns, but also normative welfare returns. The consumer benefits of improved health, from the standpoint of the fortunate beneficiaries, may considerably exceed the measurable improvements in output or income that can be attributed to it. For a penetrating theoretical and quantitative elaboration on this point, see Murphy and Topel, "The Value of Health and Longevity."

11. As two of Spain's leading economic historians have pointed out, at the end of the nineteenth century, Western Europe's investment rate (that is, gross domestic fixed capital as a proportion of gross domestic product) was about 10 percent, while today it is about 20 percent—almost exactly double the level of a century earlier. Cf. Albert Carreras and Xavier Tunafell, "Long Term Growth of the Western European Countries and the United States, 1830–2000: Facts and Issues" (lecture paper, International Economic History Association Congress, Helsinki, August 21–25, 2006), http://www.helsinki.fi/iehc2006/papers3/Carreras103.pdf (accessed June 1, 2007).

12. The scope for cost-reducing innovations may be even greater than is sometimes supposed if the "cost of death" theory suggested by some current research is substantiated. Briefly outlined, this work indicates that health and medical costs may tend to be concentrated during a patient's very last years of life. Strong versions of this theory argue that age per se is not a significant

factor in determining health and medical outlays; rather, age and medical spending tend to associate positively, since the great majority of people in Western societies today live into their seventies and eighties. Weaker versions of the theory hold that age does play a role in determining medical spending, but that the "cost of death" phenomenon nevertheless portends a dampening impact on health-care pressures in an aging society because those eventual end-of-life expenditures are being extended over a longer time horizon. For further reading in this new literature, see Peter Zweifel, Stefan Felder, and Andreas Werblow, "Population Ageing and Health Care Expenditure: New Evidence on the 'Red Herring,'" *Geneva Papers on Risk and Insurance* 29, no. 4 (October 2004): 652–66; Meena Seshamani and Alastair M. Gray, "Ageing and Health-Care Expenditure: The Red Herring Argument Revisited," *Health Economics* 13, no. 4 (2004): 303–14; Zhou Yang, Edward C. Norton, and Sally C. Stearns, "Longevity and Health Care Expenditures: The Real Reasons Older People Spend More," *Journal of Gerontology Series B: Psychological Sciences and Social Sciences* 58 (2003): S2–S10; Sarah C. Stearns and Edward C. Norton, "Time to Include Time to Death? The Future of Health Expenditure Predictions," *Health Economics* 13, no. 4 (2004): 315–27; and Brigitte Dormont, Michel Grignon, and Hélène Huber, "Health Expenditures Growth: Reassessing the Threat of Ageing," *Health Economics* 15, no. 9 (2006): 947–63.

13. Kenneth G. Manton, Gene R. Lowrimore, Arthur D. Ullian, XiLiang Gu, and H. Dennis Tolley, "Labor Force Participation and Human Capital Increases in an Aging Population and Implications for U.S. Research Investment," *Proceedings of the National Academy of Sciences* 104, no. 26 (June 26, 2007): 10802–7.

14. See European Commission, Research Directorate, *Key Figures 2007 on Science, Technology and Innovation: Towards a European Knowledge Area* (Brussels: European Union, May 11, 2007), http://ec.europa.eu/invest-in-research/pdf/kf_2007_prepub_en.pdf (accessed August 16, 2007). According to the EU's estimates, its member states allocated roughly 1.9 percent of GDP to R&D in 2005, as against 2.6 percent in the United States and 3.1 percent in Japan.

15. R. L. K. Virchow, *Die Einheitsbestrebungen in der wissenschaftlichen Medicin* (Berlin: G. Reimer, 1849), 48, cited in Paul Farmer, *Pathologies of Power: Health, Human Rights, and the New War on the Poor* (Berkeley, Calif.: University of California Press, 2003), 323 n44.

16. For a few examples of recent studies that approach health policy analysis from the perspective of minimizing the cost of illness and disease, see Richard D. Miller Jr. and H. E. Frech III, *Health Care Matters:*

Pharmaceuticals, Obesity, and the Quality of Life (Washington, D.C.: AEI Press, 2004); and Robert L. Ohsfeldt and John E. Schneider, *The Business of Health: The Role of Competition Markets and Regulation* (Washington, D.C.: AEI Press, 2006).

References

Alesina, Alberto, and Francesco Giavazzi. *The Future of Europe: Reform or Decline*. Cambridge, Mass.: MIT Press, 2006.

Alesina, Alberto, Edward Glaeser, and Bruce Sacerdote. "Work and Leisure in the U.S. and Europe: Why So Different?" Discussion Paper 2068, Harvard Institute of Economic Research, April 2005. http://econweb. fas.harvard.edu/hier/2005papers/HIER2068.pdf (accessed June 1, 2007).

Arias, Elizabeth. "United States Life Table, 2003." *National Vital Statistics Reports* 54, no. 14 (April 19, 2006). http://www.cdc.gov/nchs/data/nvsr/ nvsr54/nvsr54_14.pdf (accessed May 9, 2007).

Baily, Martin Neil, and Jacob Funk Kierkegaard. *Transforming the European Economy*. Washington, D.C.: Institute for International Economics, 2004.

Becker, Gary S., Tomas J. Philipson, and Rodrigo R. Soares. "The Quantity and Quality of Life and the Evolution of World Inequality." Working Paper 9765, National Bureau of Economic Research, Cambridge, Mass., 2003.

Bourgeois-Pichat, Jean. "Évolution générale de la population française depuis le XVIIe siècle." *Population* 6, no. 4 (1951): 635–62.

Braudel, Fernand. *L'Identité de France*, vol. 1. Paris: Arthaud-Flammarion, 1986.

Burniaux, Jean-Marc, Romain Duval, and Florence Jaumotte. "Coping with Ageing: A Dynamic Approach to Quantify the Impact of Alternative Policy Options on Future Labor Supply in OECD Countries." Working Paper 371, OECD Economics Department, 2004.

Carreras, Albert, and Xavier Tunafell. "Long Term Growth of the Western European Countries and the United States, 1830–2000: Facts and Issues." Lecture paper, International Economic History Association Congress, Helsinki, August 21–25, 2006. http://www.helsinki.fi/iehc 2006/papers3/Carreras103.pdf (accessed June 1, 2007).

Coleman, David. "Immigration and Ethnic Change in Low-Fertility Countries: A Third Demographic Transition." *Population and Development Review* 32, no. 3 (September 2006): 401–46.

Costa, Dora L. "Changing Chronic Disease Rates and Long-Term Declines in Functional Limitation among Older Men." *Demography* 39, no.1 (February 2002): 119–37.

———. "Understanding the Twentieth-Century Decline in Chronic Conditions among Older Men." *Demography* 37, no. 1 (February 2000): 53–72.

Council of Europe. *Recent Demographic Developments in Europe 2005.* Strasbourg: Council of Europe, 2006.

Dormont, Brigitte, Michel Grignon, and Hélène Huber. "Health Expenditures Growth: Reassessing the Threat of Ageing." *Health Economics* 15, no. 9 (2006): 947–63.

Dorn, David, and Alfonso Sousa-Poza. "Why is the Employment Rate of Older Swiss So High? An Analysis of the Social Security System." *European Papers on the New Welfare* 1 (2005). http://eng.newwelfare.org/ ?p=188&page=1 (accessed July 2, 2007).

Duval, Romain. "The Retirement Effects of Old-Age Pension and Early Retirement Schemes in OECD Countries." Working Paper 370, Organisation for Economic Co-operation and Development, Economics Department, Paris, France, November 2003.

European Commission, Research Directorate. *Key Figures 2007 on Science, Technology and Innovation: Towards a European Knowledge Area.* Brussels: European Union, May 11, 2007. http://ec.europa.eu/invest-in-research/ pdf/kf_2007_prepub_en.pdf (accessed August 16, 2007).

Eurostat. "First Demographic Estimates for Europe 2005." *Statistics in Focus* 1 (January 2006). http://epp.eurostat.ec.europa.eu/cache/ITY_ OFF PUB/KS-NK-06-001/EN/KS-NK-06-001-EN.PDF (accessed May 9, 2007).

———. Population Data. http://epp.eurostat.ec.europa.eu/portal/page?_ pageid=1996,45323734&_dad=portal&_schema=PORTAL&screen= welcomeref&open=/popula/proj/proj_trend&language=en&product =EU_MASTER_population&root=EU_MASTER_population&scrollto =0 (for population projections, accessed May 9, 2007).

———. "Population in Europe 2005: First Results." *Statistics in Focus* 16 (November 2006). http://epp.eurostat.ec.europa.eu/cache/ITY_OFFPUB/KS-NK-06-016/EN/KS-NK-06-016-EN.PDF (accessed May 9, 2007).

———. *Population Statistics: 2006 Edition.* Luxembourg: Eurostat, 2006.

Farmer, Paul. *Pathologies of Power: Health, Human Rights, and the New War on the Poor.* Berkeley, Calif.: University of California Press, 2003.

Feyrer, James. "Demographics and Productivity." *Review of Economics and Statistics* 89, no. 1 (January 2007): 100–109.

Fogel, Robert W. "Changes in the Disparities in Chronic Diseases during the Course of the Twentieth Century." Working Paper 10311, National Bureau of Economic Research, February 2004.

———. *The Escape from Hunger and Premature Death, 1700–2100*. New York: Cambridge University Press, 2004.

———. "Health, Nutrition and Economic Growth." *Economic Development and Cultural Change* 52, no. 3 (April 2004): 643–58.

———. "Secular Trends in Physiological Capital: Implications for Equity in Health Care." Working Paper 9771, National Bureau of Economic Research, June 2003.

Haarde, Geir H. "Strengthening Growth and Public Finances in an Era of Demographic Change." Background Paper, Organisation for Economic Co-operation and Development, Paris, France, May 13–14, 2004.

Hamilton, Brady E. "Reproduction Rates for 1990–2002 and Intrinsic Rates for 2000–2001: United States." *National Vital Statistics Reports* 52, no. 17 (March 18, 2004). http://www.cdc.gov/nchs/data/nvsr/nvsr52/nvsr52 _17.pdf (accessed May 31, 2007).

Heckman, James J., and Bas Jacobs. "Policies to Create and Destroy Human Capital in Europe." In *Perspectives on the Performance of the Continent's Economies*, ed. Hans-Werner Sinn and Edmund Phelps. Cambridge, Mass.: MIT Press, forthcoming.

Human Mortality Database. University of California, Berkeley (USA) and Max Planck Institute for Demographic Research (Germany). http://www. mortality.org (accessed December 21, 2006).

Institut National de la Statistique et des Études Économiques. "Le bilan démographique 2006—un excédent naturel record." January 16, 2007. http://www.insee.fr/fr/ffc/pop_age4.htm (accessed May 9, 2007).

International Labour Office. LABORSTA Internet. http://laborsta.ilo.org (accessed July 2, 2007).

Jones, Benjamin F. "Age and Great Invention." Working Paper 11359, National Bureau of Economic Research, May 2005. http://www.nber.org/ papers/11359 (accessed July 2, 2007).

Keese, Mark. "Ageing and Employment in Europe: A Summary of OECD Evidence and Perspectives." Report, Organisation for Economic Co-operation and Development and International Longevity Center, Paris, April 2005. http://www.ilc-france.org/actualites/docs/OECDpaper_22April .pdf (accessed May 9, 2007).

Lanzieri, Giampaolo. "Population in Europe 2005: First Results." *Statistics in Focus* 16 (November 2006), http://epp.eurostat.ec.europa.eu/cache/ITY _OFFPUB/KS-NK-06-016/EN/KS-NK-06-016-EN.PDF (accessed July 2, 2007).

Lanzieri, Giampaolo, and Veronica Corsini. "First Demographic Estimates for Europe 2005." *Statistics in Focus* 1 (January 2006), http://epp.euro stat.ec.europa.eu/cache/ITY_OFFPUB/KS-NK-06-001/EN/KS-NK-06-001-EN.PDF (accessed July 2, 2007).

Laroque, Guy, and Bernard Salinie. "Does Fertility Respond to Financial Incentives?" Discussion Paper 5007, Center for Economic Policy Research, London, April 2005.

Lee, Ronald D. *Global Population Aging and Its Economic Consequences.* Washington, D.C.: AEI Press, 2007.

Maddison, Angus. *The World Economy: Historical Statistics.* Paris: OECD, 2003.

———. "World Population, GDP and GDP Per Capita, 1–2003 AD." http://www.ggdc.net/maddison/Historical_Statistics/horizontal-file_03-2007.xls (accessed June 15, 2007).

Manton, Kenneth G., Gene R. Lowrimore, Arthur D. Ullian, XiLiang Gu, and H. Dennis Tolley. "Labor Force Participation and Human Capital Increases in an Aging Population and Implications for U.S. Research Investment." *Proceedings of the National Academy of Sciences* 104, no. 26 (June 26, 2007): 10802–7.

Miller, Richard D., Jr., and H. E. Frech III. *Health Care Matters: Pharmaceuticals, Obesity, and the Quality of Life.* Washington, D.C.: AEI Press, 2004.

Murphy, Kevin M., and Robert H. Topel. "The Value of Health and Longevity." *Journal of Political Economy* 114, no. 5 (October 2006): 871–904.

Oeppen, James, and James W. Vaupel. "Broken Limits to Life Expectancy." *Science* 296, no. 5570 (May 10, 2002): 1029–31.

Ohsfeldt, Robert L., and John E. Schneider. *The Business of Health: The Role of Competition Markets and Regulation.* Washington, D.C.: AEI Press, 2006.

Organisation for Economic Co-operation and Development. *Education at a Glance: OECD Indicators, 2002.* Paris: OECD, 2002.

———. "GDP per Capita, USP, Converted Using PPPs, 2003." http://ocde.p4.siteinternet.com/publications/doifiles/012004071B0G002.xls (accessed June 15, 2007).

———. *Labour Force Statistics 1985–2005.* Paris: OECD, 2006.

———. *Live Longer, Work Longer.* Paris: OECD, 2006.

———. *Society at a Glance: OECD Social Indicators, 2005 Edition.* Paris: OECD, 2005.

Pritchett, Lant H., and Lawrence H. Summers. "Wealthier Is Healthier." *Journal of Human Resources* 31, no. 4 (Autumn 1996): 841–68.

Rau, Roland, Eugeny Soroko, Domantas Jasilionis, and James W. Vaupel. "Ten Years after Kannisto: Further Evidence for Mortality Decline at

Advanced Ages in Developed Countries." Working Paper 2006-033, Max Planck Institute for Demographic Research, October 2006.

Rudaz, Jean-François. "Einfluss des Gesundheitszustandes auf den Altersrücktritt." *Die Volkswirtschaft* (Bern), no. 10 (2005). http://www.smd.ch/faksimile/f200510/vow_20051001_1005_1_1.pdf (accessed May 31, 2007).

Sapir, André, Philippe Aghion, Giuseppe Bertola, Martin Hellwig, Jean Pisani-Ferry, Dariusz Rosati, José Viñals, and Helen Wallace. *An Agenda for a Growing Europe: The Sapir Report.* New York: Oxford University Press, 2004.

Sarkozy, Nicholas. "Démographie et politique." *Agir* (Paris) 29 (January 2007): 15–20.

Scherer, Peter. *Age of Withdrawal from the Labour Force in OECD Countries.* Occasional Paper 49, Labor Market and Social Policy, Organisation for Economic Co-operation and Development, Paris, France, January 11, 2002.

Schultz, T. Paul. "Human Capital and Development." In *Agricultural Competitiveness*, ed. G. H. Peters et al. Aldershot, England: Dartmouth Publishing Group, 1995.

Seshamani, Meena, and Alastair M. Gray. "Ageing and Health-Care Expenditure: The Red Herring Argument Revisited." *Health Economics* 13, no. 4 (2004): 303–14.

Skirbegg, Vigard. "Age and Individual Productivity: A Literature Survey." Working Paper WP-2003-028, Max Planck Institute for Demographic Research, August 2003. http://www.demogr.mpg.de/papers/working/wp-2003-028.pdf (accessed May 9, 2007).

Soldo, Beth J., Olivia S. Mitchell, Rania Tfaily, and John F. McCabe. "Cross-Cohort Differences on the Verge of Retirement." Working Paper 12762, National Bureau of Economic Research, December 2006.

SourceOECD. *Employment and Labour Market Statistics.* http://www.source oecd.org (accessed July 27, 2007).

———. *National Accounts Statistics.* http://www.sourceoecd.org (accessed August 30, 2006).

Stearns, Sarah C., and Edward C. Norton. "Time to Include Time to Death? The Future of Health Expenditure Predictions." *Health Economics* 13, no. 4 (2004): 315–27.

Thierry, Xavier. "Avenir des migrations européennes: Regard critique sur les projections des Nations Unies." *Agir* (Paris) 29 (January 2007): 54–62.

Tribalat, Michèle. "Vers un sélectivité et un contrôle accrus des politiques migratoires en Europe." *Agir* (Paris) 29 (January 2007): 33–44.

U.S. Census Bureau. "United States Foreign-Born Population." http://www.census.gov/population/www/socdemo/foreign/datatbls.html (accessed February 21, 2007).

————. International Data Base, http:www.census.gov/cgi-bin/ipc/idbagg (accessed June 1, 2007).

————. International Programs Center. International Data Base. http://www. census.gov/ipc/www/idbnew.html (for total midyear population; accessed August 16, 2007).

United Nations Educational, Scientific and Cultural Organization (UNESCO). *International Standard Classification of Education: ISCED 1997*, 34–38. http://www.uis.unesco.org/TEMPLATE/pdf/isced/ISCED _A.pdf (accessed July 3, 2007).

United Nations Population Division. World Population Prospects: The 2006 Revision Population Database. http://esa.un.org/unpp/ (accessed June 1, 2007).

University of California, Berkeley, and Max Planck Institute for Demographic Research. Human Mortality Database. http://www.mortality.org (accessed December 21, 2006).

Van Dalen, Hendrik P., and Kene Henkens. "Longing for the Good Life: Understanding Emigration from a High-Income Country." *Population and Development Review* 33, no. 1 (March 2007): 37–65.

Vaupel, James W., and Elke Loichinger. "Redistributing Work in Aging Europe." *Science* 312, no. 5782 (June 30, 2006): 1911–13.

Vaupel, James W., James R. Carey, Kaare Christensen, Thomas E. Johnson, Anatoli I. Yashin, Niels V. Holm, Ivan A. Iachine, Väinö Kannisto, Aziz A. Khazaeli, Pablo Liedo, Valter D. Lango, Yi Zeng, Kenneth G. Manton James W. Curtsinger. "Biodemographic Trajectories of Longevity." *Science* 280, no. 5365 (May 8, 1998): 855–60.

World Bank. *World Development Indicators, 2003*. Washington, D.C.: World Bank, 2003.

Yang, Zhou, Edward C. Norton, and Sally C. Stearns. "Longevity and Health Care Expenditures: The Real Reasons Older People Spend More." *Journal of Gerontology Series B: Psychological Sciences and Social Sciences* 58 (2003): S2–S10.

Ziegler, Uta, and Gabriela Dolbhammer. "Steigende Lebenserwartung geht mit besserer Gesundheit einher: Risiko der Pflegebedürftigkeit in Deutschland sinkt." *Demografische Forschung aus Erster Hand* 2, no. 1 (January 2005). http://www.demografische-forschung.org/archiv/defo 0501.pdf (accessed July 2, 2007).

Zweifel, Peter, Stefan Felder, and Andreas Werblow. "Population Ageing and Health Care Expenditure: New Evidence on the 'Red Herring.'" *Geneva Papers on Risk and Insurance* 29, no. 4 (October 2004): 652–66.

About the Authors

Nicholas Eberstadt is the Henry Wendt Scholar in Political Economy at the American Enterprise Institute (AEI), and is senior adviser to the National Bureau of Asian Research (NBR). He has served on the Board of Scientific Counselors for the U.S. National Center for Health Statistics, and is currently a member of the President's Council on Bioethics. Mr. Eberstadt's previous books on health and demographic issues include *Fertility Decline in the Less Developed Countries* (editor, 1981), *The Tyranny of Numbers* (1995), *Prosperous Paupers and Other Population Problems* (2000), and *Health and the Income Inequality Hypothesis* (coauthor, 2004). Mr. Eberstadt earned his AB, MPA, and PhD from Harvard University, and his MSc from the London School of Economics.

Hans Groth, MD, is a member of the Board of Directors of Pfizer Switzerland. He holds an MD from the Universities of Marburg (Germany) and Zurich (Switzerland) and an MBA from Henley Management College (England), and he has eighteen years of extensive industry experience in numerous European and overseas markets. In 2003, in his capacity as a Pfizer Global Health Fellow, he conducted HIV/AIDS epidemiological field research in Siberia and Central Asia on behalf of UNAIDS. Since then, he has been personally committed to supporting HIV harm-reduction projects in the Lake Baikal region of Siberia. Inspired by these experiences, Dr. Groth has developed a deep interest in the "health-wealth relationship" in light of global demographic changes and their implications for the economic, social, and political agendas, which need to be addressed by all nations.